French Language Learning

Your Beginner's Guide to Easily Learn French While in Your Car or Working Out!

Language Learning Mastery

Table of Contents

Introduction

If you're looking for a book that can guarantee an easy but effective way to learn French, then look no more.

This book contains an in-depth guide about the French grammar explained simply and illustrated with lots of examples. Delving into grammar may be daunting (or boring) but it's the only way to fully learn a language and understand how every word functions to form something that makes sense. Sure, you can memorize a lot of words and phrases but remember: what you understand, you will never forget.

A lot of people who are just beginning to learn French are put off by the complex pronunciation of the words. In this book, a pronunciation guide for most of the examples are stated so you're sure that you don't just learn a word. You also know how to say it the right way.

If you're learning French because you're planning to visit France, you don't need to wait until you master the language before booking that flight because this book's got you covered. The vast collection of words and expressions included in this book will not only help you navigate the day-to-day situations in the French-speaking world. It will also make sure that you get more out of your trip.

Thanks for downloading this book, I hope you enjoy it!

Chapter 1: Pronunciation and the French Alphabet

It's quite normal to get intimidated hearing French people talk. But you don't need to feel like that for long.

People who can play any musical instrument or carry a tune will find it easy to copy the stress and intonation of the language. But even if you're not born with a good ear, there's no need to worry. Simply follow these tips:

- Lose your inhibitions. Imitate not just the sound but also the body language and facial expressions of native French speakers. There's no such thing as exaggeration when putting on your best French accent.

- Use your nose wisely. Unlike English, the French language has nasal vowels, which are created by expelling air through the nose.

- Start small. Learn how to pronounce individual letters before moving on to more complicated words.

- Be patient. It takes time to learn any language. Practice regularly and devote sufficient time to improve your accent.

Individual Sounds

The same alphabet is used in the French and English languages. However, the way letters are pronounced, particularly vowels, is rather different.

Vowels

With each one having several different sounds, French vowels are a bit complicated. Knowing the rules and how accent marks work will help you decide how a specific vowel is pronounced.

Letter	Symbol	Pronunciation Guide
a à â	ah	Say **a** as in **father** and **spa**, but open your mouth wider. Ex: façade *fah-sahd* (façade)
e – in a single-syllable word or in the middle of a word and followed by just one consonant	uh	Say **e** as in **the.** Ex: le *luh* (the) leçon *luh-soh* (lesson)
é	ay	Say **ay** as in **stay.** Ex: liberté *lee-behr-tay*
è ê	eh	Say **e** as in **met.** Ex: après ah-preh (after) fête *feht* (feast)
i y	ee	Say **i** as in **medicine.** Ex: ami *ah-mee* (friend)
o – followed by se, the word	o	Say **o** as in **nose.** Your lips should be rounded.

itself, last pronounced sound of a word ô		Ex: nos *no* (our)
o – followed by a pronounced consonant other than s	oh	Say **o** as in **glove.** Ex: homme *ohm* (man)
u û	ew	No equivalent. Ex: plus *plew* (more)

Note:

- **Y** is treated as a vowel in the French language. **H** may or may not be a vowel.

- The sound of *u* doesn't exist in English and is unique to the French language. To pronounce it, round your lips and try saying the sound *oo* while saying *ee*.

Consonants

When consonants occur at the end of a French word, they are generally not pronounced. Think of the word "careful" when you encounter a word ending in a consonant. If the final letter isn't *c, r, f,* or *l,* you usually don't pronounce it. You may be tempted to pronounce the final *s.* Never fall for it.

Letter	Symbol	Pronunciation Guide
b, d, f, k, l, m, n, p, s, t, v, z	Same	Same pronunciation as English.
c – before a, u, o, or any consonant q - final	k	Say the **c** as in **card.** Ex: clé *klay* (key)
c – before e, i, or y ç s – at beginning of word or next to a consonant t – before i + vowel	s	Say the **c** as in **cent.** Ex: cette *seht* (this, that) ça va sah vah (okay) salut sah-lewt (hi, bye) aristocratie *ah-rees-toh-krah-see* (aristocracy)
g – before a, o, u, or a consonant	g	Say the **g** as in **go.** Ex: gris *gree* (gray)
g – before e, i, or y j	zh	Say the **s** as in **pleasure.** Ex: neige *nehzh* (snow) jaune *zhon* (yellow)
h		Always silent Ex: hiver *ee-vehr* (winter)
s – between vowels	z	Say **z** as in **zone.** Ex: musée *mew-zay* (museum)

Note:

- **X** at the end of a word is silent with the exception of these two words:

dix	*dees*	*ten*
six	*sees*	*six*

- Careful with "careful" because there's always an exception to a rule.

-**er** at the end of a word is pronounced as **ay**.

parler	*pahr-lay*	to speak
boulanger	*boo-lahn-zhay*	baker

Below are words ending in **c**, **r**, **f**, and **l** but their final consonant shouldn't be pronounced.

banc	*bahN*	bench
blanc	*blahN*	white
estomac	*ehs-toh-mah*	stomach
franc	*frahN*	frank
gentil	*zhahN-tee*	kind
nerf	*nehr*	nerve
outil	*ooh-tee*	tool
porc	*pohr*	pork
tabac	*tah-bah*	tobacco

- Pronounce the ending consonant of the words listed below.

as	*ahs*	ace
cap	*kahp*	cape
coq	*kohk*	rooster

fils	*fees*	son
maïs	*mah-ees*	corn
net	*neht*	clear
oust	*wehst*	west
sud	*sewd*	south

- Pronounce the final consonant of foreign words that are incorporated in the French language. A few examples are **internet, sandwich, tennis, and parking.**

Combined Letters

Combining vowels and consonants create new sounds which may be quite unlike how they sound on their own. There are several combinations possible: a two- or three-vowel sequence, a consonant and vowel, or two consonants.

Letter Combination	Symbol	Pronunciation Guide
er and ez – final es – in a few one-syllable words ai – limited to some words	ay	Say **ay** as in **stay.** Ex: nez *nay* (nose) les *lay* (the)
ui	ee	Say **i** as in **medicine.** Ex: minuit *mee-nwee* (midnight)
i + ll il – when preceded by a vowel	y	Say **y** as in **yesterday.** Ex: travailler *trah-vah-yay* (to work) ail *ahy* (garlic)
au eau	o	Say **o** as in **nose.**

10

		Ex: chaussettes *sho-seht* (socks) ciseaux *see-zo* (scissors)
ou où oû	oo	Say **oo** as in **booth**. Ex: court *koor* short
oi oy	wah	Say **w** as in **water**. Ex: noir *nwahr* (black) voyager *vwah-yah-zhay* (to travel)
ch	sh	Say the **ch** as in **machine**. Ex: cher *shehr* (dear, expensive)
gn	ny	Say the **n** as in **union**. Ex: gagner *gah-nyay* (to earn)
th	t	Say **t** as in **time**. Ex: thé *tay* (tea)

Note:

- A vowel sound is always produced even when a consonant is combined with a vowel.

- There's no *th* sound in French.

The Letter R

The French **r** is infamous. Pronouncing it isn't that easy. Unlike in English, it requires your throat to get involved.

To pronounce **r** the way the French do, lower your tongue to the floor of your mouth and keep it pressed against your teeth. When you say **r**, do it as if you're gargling or clearing your throat.

Remember not to roll your **r**; that's Spanish. Don't roll your tongue as well; that's English.

Nasal Sounds

When **n** or **m** is preceded by a vowel and they're in the same syllable, a nasal sound is followed. In the pronunciation text, this is represented by **N**.

Letter Combination	Symbol	Pronunciation Guide
an (am) en (em)	ahN	Ex: étranger *ay-trahN-zhay* (foreign) enfant *ahn-fahN* (child)
in (im) ain (aim)	aN	Ex: vin *vaN* (wine) maintenant *maNt-nahN* (now)
oin	waN	Ex: loin *lwaN* (far)
ien	yaN	Ex: bien sûr *byaN sewr* (of course)
on (om)	ohN	Ex: avion *ah-vyohN* (airplane)
un (um)	uhN	Ex: brun *bruhN* (brunette, brown)

Accent Marks

One thing that differentiates the English from the French alphabet is the use of accent marks in the latter. Five different accent marks are applied in French. They are primarily used to change how a letter is pronounced. They are useful in differentiating between two words with the same spelling but completely different meaning. They are also used to replace an s in Old French.

- aigu or acute (´) – applied only on an e (é)

    If you try to mentally put s in place of é at the beginning of a word, you may be able to easily figure out what that word means. For example: étranger (stranger) and éponge (sponge).

- grave (`) – applied on a (à), e (è) and u (ù)

- circumflex (^) – may be applied on all vowels.

    The circumflex also substitutes s from old French although the resulting word is a bit different. For example: fête (festival, feast) and arrêter (arrest).

- cedilla (¸) – applied only on c followed by a, e, or u

- trema (¨) – applied on a second vowel in a series. This specifies that the two vowels are pronounced distinctly.

Stress

In French, only the last syllable of a word is emphasized. Each preceding syllable is given equal emphasis. This is quite different from English where stress placement depends on the word itself. For that reason, predicting word stress when you're encountering new French words each time will be stress-free.

American	Ameri**cain**
Mexican	Mexi**cain**
Medite**rra**nean	Méditerran**ee**

French speakers treat a group of words like a single word. When words are chained together to form phrases or sentences, only the syllable of the last word is emphasized. If you don't drop the stress in each word, you may not be understood.

We are **vi**siting the **cathe**dral.	Nous visitons la cathé**drale**.
He is for**bid**den to cheat.	Il est défendu de tri**cher**.
Stress **con**tributes to **ma**ny **ill**nesses.	Le stress contribute à beaucoup de mala**dies**.

Liaison and Elision

Two linguistic elements that make the French language fluid and melodic are liaison and elision.

In the French language, the final consonant of a word is linked to the beginning vowel or vowel sound (commonly, h and y) of the next word. This practice is called liaison or linking.

Here are the most common combinations of letters linked by the liaison:

- S or x producing a z sound

vous arrivez	*voo-zah-ree-vay*
len enfant	*lay-zahN-fahN*

- D or t producing a t sound

petit enfant	*puh-tee tan-fahN*
grand arbre	*grahN-tahr-br*

- N producing an n sound

on aime	*ohN-nehm*
un étudiant	*uhN-nay-tew-dee-ahN*

And here are liaisons which occur less frequently:

- P producing a p sound

beaucoup aime	*boh-kooh-peh-may*

- F followed by the words **an** or **heure** producing a v sound

neuf heure	*nuh-vuhr*
neuf ans	*nuh-vahN*

Note: You may be tempted to use the liaison each time you see these letter combinations. However, you can't do it every single time you see a word ending in a consonant followed by a word starting with a vowel. Here are the instances where you shouldn't use liaison.

- A noun followed by an adjective

- The first word is **et**

- The first word is a proper noun

- A plural noun followed by a verb

- **ils**, **elles**, or **on** and a past-participle

15

- The first word is an interrogative word except for these two fixed phrases: **Comment allez-vous?** and any question starting with **quand est-ce que**

Elision or sliding usually occurs when pronounced vowel sounds occur at the end of a word and the beginning of the succeeding word. Drop the last vowel, add an apostrophe, and slide the two words together.

| je + imite | j'imite | zhee-meet |
| le + hôpital | l'hôpital | lo-pee-tahl |

Chapter 2: Numbers, Dates, and Time

Whether we like it or not, numbers will always be part of our daily lives. They're necessary in a lot of the things we do. Aside from counting, we use numbers to tell the date and time, and more.

Cardinal Numbers

Numbers denoting quantity are called cardinal numbers. They're whole numbers that we use for counting.

Let's start from 0 to 16. We can call this group the base numbers. Later on you will see that these numbers are repeated or combined to form larger numbers.

French word	Pronunciation	Number
zéro	*zay-ro*	0
un	*uhN*	1
deux	*duh*	2
trois	*trwah*	3
quatre	*kahtr*	4
cinq	*saNk*	5
six	*sees*	6
sept	*seht*	7
huit	*weet*	8
neuf	*nuhf*	9
dix	*dees*	10
onze	*ohNz*	11
douze	*dooz*	12
treize	*trehz*	13
quatorze	*kah-tohrz*	14
quinze	*kaNz*	15
seize	*sehz*	16

Note that the numbers 11 to 16 have similarity to numbers 1 to 6. The pronunciation is slightly changed and they end with **-ze**.

dix-sept	*dee-seht*	17
dix-huit	*dee-zweet*	18
dix-neuf	*dee-nuhf*	19

Between 20 and 69, you only need to memorize the tens numbers (20, 30, 40, 50, 60). Forming the other numbers follow the same pattern. Simply combine the tens numbers with the ones numbers (1 to 9). In written form, they are joined by a hypen.

vingt	*vaN*	20
vingt et un	*vaN-tay-uhN*	21
vingt-deux	*vaN-duh*	22
vingt-troix	*vaN- trwah*	23
vingt-quatre	*vaN- kahtr*	24
vingt-cinq	*vaN-saNk*	25
vingt-six	*vaN-sees*	26
vingt-sept	*vaN-seht*	27
vingt-huit	*vaN-weet*	28
vingt-neuf	*vaN-nuhf*	29
trente	*trahNt*	30
quarante	*kah-rahNt*	40
cinquante	*saN-kahNt*	50
soixante	*swah-sahNt*	60

The numbers from 70 to 99 follow a completely different pattern.

69 is *soixante-neuf* and in English is literally sixty-nine. However, when you reach 70, it becomes *soixante-dix* – sixty-ten. You're basically adding the combined numbers: 60 + 10 = 70.

The next nine numbers follow this pattern which means 71 is sixty-eleven (60 + 11), 72 is sixty-twelve (60 + 12) and so on.

soixante-dix	*swah-sahNt-dees*	70
soixante et onze	*swah-sahNt-ay-ohNz*	71
soixante-douze	*swah-sahNt-dooz*	72
soixante-treize	*swah-sahNt-trehz*	73
soixante-quatorze	*swah-sahNt-kah-tohrz*	74
soixante-quinze	*swah-sahNt-kaNz*	75
soixante-seize	*swah-sahNt-sehz*	76
soixante-dix-sept	*swah-sahNt-dee-seht*	77
soixante-dix-huit	*swah-sahNt-dee-zweet*	78
soixante-dix-neuf	*swah-sahNt-dee-znuhf*	79

80 is *quatre-vingts* or four-twenties (4 x 20 = 80).

quatre-vingts	*kahtr-vaN*	80
quatre-vingt-un	*kahtr-vaN-uhN*	81
quatre-vingt-deux	*kahtr-vaN-duh*	82
quatre-vingt-neuf	*kathr-vaN-nuhf*	89

Instead of a new word for 90, the same base of 80 is used. 90 is eighty-ten (80 + 10), 91 is eighty-eleven (80 + 11), and so forth.

quatre-vingt-dix	*kahtr-vaN-dees*	90
quatre-vingt-onze	*kahtr-vaN-onze*	91
quatre-vingt-douze	*kahtr-vaN-dooz*	92
quatre-vingt-dix-neuf	*kahtr-vaN-dee-znuhf*	99

100 in French is cent. To form the next numbers, simply combine it with the first 99 numbers but don't add *et* or a hyphen between them.

cent	*sahN*	100
cent un	*sahN-uhN*	101
cent deux	*sahN-dux*	102

For numbers by the hundreds, combine the ones numbers with *cents*. If another number follows, drop the **-s** in *cents*.

deux cents	*duh-sahN*	200
deux cent un	*duh-sahN-uhN*	201
trois cents	*trwah-sahN*	300
trois cent cinquante	*trwah-sahN-saN-kahNt*	350

Mille is the French word for thousand. As with *cent*, it doesn't use *et* or a hyphen when combined with other numbers. However, *mille* doesn't change in plural form and never takes an **-s**.

mille	*meel*	1000
mille un	*meel-uhN*	1001
mille deux	*meel-duh*	1002
deux mille	*duh-meel*	2000
trois mille	*trwah-meel*	3000

Finally, here's the list of really large numbers.

un million	*uhN-meel-yohN*	1,000,000
deux millions	*duh-meel-yohN*	2,000,000
un milliard	*uhN-meel-yahr*	1,000,000,000
deux milliards	*duh-meel-yahr*	2,000,000,000
un billion	*uhN-beel-yohN*	one trillion
un billiard	*uhN-beel-yahr*	one quadrillion

Note:

- The only cardinal number that must agree with the gender of the noun that follows it is *un*.

- For numbers ending in 1, except 81 and 91, the conjunction *et* (and) is used to combine words instead of a hyphen.

- Don't use *un* before *mille* and *cent*.

Ordinal Numbers

To put things in order, you need the help of ordinal numbers. Except for *premier* and *second*, create a French ordinal number by adding *-ième* to the cardinal number.

French	Pronunciation	English
premier / première	*pruh-myay / pruh-myehr*	1st
deuxième / second(e)	*duh-zyehm / suh-gohN(d)*	2nd
troisième	*trwah-zyehm*	3rd
quatrième	*kah-tree-yehm*	4th
cinquième	*saN-kyehm*	5th
sixième	*see-zyehm*	6th
septième	*seh-tyehm*	7th
huitième	*wee-tyehm*	8th
neuvième	*nuh-vyehm*	9th
dixième	*dee-zyehm*	10th
onzième	*ohN-zyehm*	11th
douzième	*doo-zyehm*	12th
vingtième	*vaN-tyehm*	20th
centième	*sahN-tyehm*	100th

Note:

- For *quatre*, drop the silent *e* before adding *-ième*. Add *u* in *cinq* and replace *f* with *v* in *neuf*.

- *Second(e)* is typically used only in a series that's no more than two.

- The only ordinal numbers that need to agree with the gender of the nouns they describe are *premier* and *second*.

- Elision is not applied to *huitième* and *onzième*.

- To abbreviate in French, add *e* to the number, like this: 3e, 10e, 25e. This is applicable to all except for one. In case of *premier/première*, write 1er or 1ère.

- Just like in English, ordinal numbers are used when saying the denominator of fractions. 1/5 is *un cinquième*. 3/10 *troix dixièmes*. The only exceptions are:

     1/2 – *un demi*
     1/3 – *un tiers*
     1/4 - *un quart*

Dates

To talk about dates, you need more than just numbers. You also have to know the names of days and months.

Days of the Week

Unlike in English, Monday is the start of the French week. Days of the week (*les jours de la semaine*) are not capitalized unless they're used at the beginning of a sentence.

English	French	Pronunciation
Monday	lundi	luhN-dee
Tuesday	mardi	mahr-dee
Wednesday	mercredi	mehr-kruh-dee
Thursday	jeudi	zhuh-dee
Friday	vendredi	vahN-druh-dee
Saturday	samedi	sahm-dee
Sunday	dimanche	dee-mahNsh

When the definite article *le* (the) is placed before the name of a day, its meaning becomes *every* or *on*.

le mercredi	every Wednesday
le vendredi	on Fridays

Months

Months (*mois*) of the year are always written in lowercase unless they're at the beginning of a sentence. They never follow an article.

English	French	Pronunciation
January	janvier	zhahN-vee-yay
February	février	fay-vree-yay
March	mars	mahrs
April	avril	ah-vreel
May	mai	meh
June	juin	zhwaN
July	juillet	zhwee-eh
August	août	oo(t)
September	septembre	sehp-tahNbr
October	octobre	ohk-tohbr
November	novembre	noh-vahNbr
December	décembre	day-sahNbr

Dates in French are expressed using the following formula:

day of week + *le* + a cardinal number + month + year
dimanche le 20 janvier 2019

- Cardinal numbers are used to express the specific date except for one. Use *premier* for the first day of the month instead.

- Numerical abbreviation of dates is different. The order of the day and month is reversed. For example, 12/25/2019 is written as 25/12/2019 in French.

Time

In France, the 24-hr clock is more commonly used, particularly in travel schedule. In this section, you'll be able to tell time in both the 12-hour and 24-hour systems.

Quelle heure est-il?	What time is it?
A quelle heure?	At what time?

12-hour Clock

Telling time in French is a little different from how you do it in English, even when you're using the 12-hour clock.

- Use *il est* + number + *heure(s)* to tell the time on the hour.

Il est une heure.	*eel-eh-tewn-nuhr*	It's 1:00
Il est troix heure.	*eel-eh-trois-zuhr*	It's 3:00.

Note that *une* is used instead of *un* because *heure* is feminine.

- Add the number of minutes after the hour if it's less than or equal to 30 minutes.

Il est deux heures cinq.	eel-eh-duh-zuhr-saNk	It's 2:05.
Il est trois heures vingt-cinq.	eel-eh-trwah-zuhr-vaN-saNk	It's 3:25.

- If the number of minutes is greater than 30, say the next hour and use *moins* (minus). The number of minutes that you express should be subtracted from 60.

Il est quatre heures moins dix.	eel-eh-kahtr-urh-mwaN-dees	It's 4:50.
Il est cinq heures moins vingt.	eel-eh-sank-zuhr-mwaN-vaN	It's 5:40.

- For 15, 30, and 45 minutes, use the following examples:

Il est six heures et quart.	eel-eh-see-zurh-ay-kahr	It's 6:15.
Il est sept heures et demie.	eel-eh-she-tuhr-ay-duh-mee	It's 7:30.
Il est huit heures moins le quart.	eel-eh-wee-tuhr-mwaN-luh-kahr	It's 8:45.

- When using the 12-hr clock, use the following phrases to avoid confusion:

du matin	dew-mah-taN	in the morning or a.m
de l'après-midi	day-lah-preh-mee-dee	in the afternoon or p.m.
du soir	dew-swah	in the evening/night

- When telling time, always add the word *heures*. The only exception is when you're using *midi* (noon) or *minuit* (midnight).

Il est midi moins cinq.	*eel-eh-mee-dee-mwaN-saNk*	It's 11:55 a.m.
Il est minuit.	*eel-eh- mee-nwee*	It's midnight

- Use the letter *h* instead of a colon when writing time in numerical form. For example: *3h35*.

24-hour Clock

Expressing time using the 24-hr clock is quite simple. If you're not familiar with it, this system starts at *zero heure* (midnight) and ends at 23.59 (11:59 p.m.). Instead of placing *h* between the hour and minute, you write a period. There's no need for *du matin, de l'après-midi,* or *du soir* because it's already clear that once you get past 12, it's p.m.

Time Expressions

Sometimes, you need to express time not in terms of hour of the day. Here are some of the most important time-related words and expressions.

English	French	*Pronunciation*
ago	il y a ...	*eel-yah*
a day	un jour	*uhN-zhoor*
a month	un mois	*uhN-mwah*
a week	un semaine	*uhN-suh-mehn*
a year	une année	*ewn-ah-nay*
during	pendant ...	*pahN-dahN*
from	dés ...	*dahN*
last	dernier (dernière)	*dehr-nyah (dehr-nyehr)*

26

next	prochain(e)	*proh-shaN (pro-shehn)*
the day after tomorrow	après-demain	*ah-preh-duh-maN*
the day before yesterday	avant-hier	*ah-vahN-yehr*
the next day	le lendemain	*luh-lahN-duh-maN*
today	aujourd'hui	*oh-zhoor-dwee*
tomorrow	demain	*duh-maN*
yesterday	hier	*yehr*

Note: In English, the word time has a wide variety of meanings. In French, *le temps (luh-than)* can only refer to the weather (Quel temps fait-il? / What's the weather like?) and time as in, We don't have time for that. (Nous n'avons pas le temps pour ça.) For other context, choose from the following words:

Quell *heure* est-il?	What time is it?
deux *fois*	two times
souvent	many times
au moment de	at the time of
à l'époque de	in the times of

Chapter 3: The Parts of Speech

To be able to speak French - or any language - like a native, you don't have to memorize pages of rules and translate sentences word for word. The key is to understand how the words function and to recognize a language's natural patterns. To achieve that, you have to learn some basic grammar.

French grammar is a little bit complicated. But to make learning a language easier, you have to get to know what it's made of. You must be familiar with the parts of speech – the types of words that form a language – and how they work.

Just like in English, there are eight parts of speech in the French language: noun, pronoun, adjective, verb, adverb, preposition, conjunction, and interjection.

Nouns

Un nom (noun) may refer to people, things, places, or concepts.

- It functions either as a subject or an object of a verb in a sentence.

    as a subject: Le **bébé** a été vaccine. (The **baby** has been vaccinated.)
    as an object: Je fais une **soupe**. (I'm making a **soup**.)

- It has singular and plural forms.

    la **fille** vs les **filles** (daughter)

- French nouns have gender. It's either feminine or masculine.

avocat vs **avocate** (lawyer)

Pronouns

To avoid repetition, *un pronom* (a pronoun) takes the place of a noun in a sentence. A pronoun must match the number, gender, and function of the noun it replaces.

Adjectives

Le adjective (an adjective) is used to describe a noun. Articles - the short but essential words that introduce a noun such as **le, une,** and **du** – are adjectives.

To use an adjective in French correctly, you must know these two things:

- It must match the number and gender of the of the noun it modifies.

- Unlike in English, most French adjectives are placed after the noun.

un voitre **noir** (a black car)

Verbs

Les verbes (verbs) indicate a state of being or an action. They are the core element of a sentence. Indeed, you can't make a proper sentence without including a verb. Depending on the form it takes, a verb can tell what action is performed, who performs it, and when it's performed.

Verbs don't have gender but based on their infinitive form, regular verbs can be grouped into three types: the *-er*, *-ir*, and *-re* verbs.

Adverbs

Les adverbs (adverbs) are words that describe verbs, adjectives, and other adverbs. Most of the adverbs in the English language end in -ly. In French, they end in *-ment*: for example, *lentement* (slowly) and *sérieusement* (seriously).

Prepositions

A *preposition* shows a relationship of space, time, direction, or manner between a noun and another word in a sentence. Below is a list of common prepositions which you will find helpful.

after	après	*ah-preh*	from	de	*duh*
against	contre	*kohNtr*	in	dans	*dahN*
at, to	à	*ah*	in	en	*ahN*
at the house of	chez	*shay*	in front of	devant	*duh-vahN*
after	après	*ah-preh*	near	près (de)	*preh (duh)*
behind	derrière	*deh-ryehr*	on	sur	*sewr*
between	entre	*ahNtr*	toward	vers	*vehr*
by, through	par	*pahr*	under	sous	*soo*
far (from)	loin (de)	*lwaN (duh)*	with	avec	*ah-vehk*
for, in order to	pour	*poor*	without	sans	*sahN*

In English, a preposition can have a different meaning depending on the word that surrounds it. In contrast, French prepositions retain their meaning. For example, you can see in the list above that there are two words for in: *dans* and *en*. *Dans* is generally used when expressing the length of time before an action will happen. On the other hand, *en* is used to indicate the amount of time an action occurs.

Conjuctions

Words that connect grammatically connected words, phrases, or sentences are called *les conjonctions* (conjunctions). Some French conjunctions are *et* (and), *ou* (or), *mais* (but), *ni* (neither...nor), *car* (because), and *si* (if).

Interjections

Words or phrases that are used to express strong feelings or emotions are called interjections. The list of common interjections below are informal words but using them will make you sound like a native French speaker.

Beurk! / Berk!	Yuck!	Miam miam!	Yum!
Boum!	Boom! / Bang!	Mince! /Zut!	Darn!
Chiche!	Go ahead! / I dare you!	Ouf!	Phew!
Chut!	Be quiet! / Shush!	Ouïe!	Ouch!
Oh là là!	Wow!	Oups!	Oops!
Holà!	Hey!	Putain!	(general French swear word)
Hop là!	Got it!	Toc, toc!	Knock knock!
Merde!	Shit! / Break a	Youpi!	Yay!

	leg!		

Chapter 4: Nouns

In English and French, nouns name people, places, and things. They can be replaced by pronouns and have singular and plural forms. The huge difference is that in French, nouns have a gender. Everything from a tiny insect to an enormous ship is classified as either feminine or masculine.

Gender

If you're speaking about a man or a woman, or any other living being with gender, it's quite obvious whether it is masculine or feminine. The tricky part is when nouns refer to objects, places, or concepts. It doesn't follow any logic but there are a few patterns that can help you identify the gender of nouns.

Note: In a dictionary, "*f.*" and "*m.*" are used to indicate a feminine and masculine word, respectively.

Noun Identifiers

Short articles work as noun identifiers. Usually they can help you distinguish both gender and number.

There are 3 types of articles. These are definite, indefinite and partitive. For now, let's look at only the first two.

Singular Noun Markers	Feminine	Masculine
the (definite)	la (l') *luh*	le (l') *luh*
a, an, one (indefinite)	une *ewn*	un *uhN*

A number of nouns have the same feminine and masculine form. Their gender depends on whether the speaker refers to a female or male.

	Feminine	Masculine
an artist	une artiste	un artiste
an athlete	une athlete	un athlète
a child	une enfant	un enfant
a sick person	la malade	le malade
a tourist	la touriste	le touriste

Fixed Gender Nouns

Some nouns are always feminine or masculine regardless of the sex of the being it refers to.

Always Feminine			Always Masculine		
connaissance	*koh-neh-sahNs*	acquaintance	professeur	*proh-feh-suhr*	teacher
personne	*pehr-sohn*	person	dentiste	*dahN-teest*	dentist
vedette	*vuh-deht*	start	médecin	*mayd-saN*	doctor
victime	*veek-teem*	victim	bébé	*bay-bay*	baby

Note: Le *professeur* is used for middle school, high school, and college teachers. For an elementary school teacher, use *l'instituter.*

If you're referring to a male using a word that is always feminine, add the word *homme* (man) before the feminine noun. If you're talking about a female with a masculine noun, add the word *femme* (woman).

une femme dentist   un homme connaissance

Identifying Feminine Nouns

You can spot many feminine nouns based on their endings.

Noun Ending	Examples		
-ade	ambassade	*ahN-bah-sahd*	embassy
-ale	carte postale escale	*kahrt-pohs-tahl* *ehs-kahl*	post card stopover
-ance	quittance	*kee-tahNs*	receipt
-ée	entrée	*ahN-tray*	entrance
-ence	essence	*eh-sahNs*	gasoline
-ette	assiette chaussette étiquitte	*ah-syeht* *sho-seht* *ay-tee-keht*	dinner plate sock identification tag
-ie	blanchiesserie confiserie librairie	*blahN-shees-ree* *kohN-feez-ree* *lee-breh-ree*	laundry and dry cleaning service candy store bookstore
-ique	boutique	*boo-teek*	gift shop
-oire	histoire	*ess-twahr*	history
-sion	climatisation télévision	*klee-mah-tee-zah-syohN* *tay-lay-vee-*	air conditioning television

		zyohN	
-té	société	*soh-syee-tay*	society
	charité	*sha-ree-tay*	charity
-tié	amitié	*ah-mee-tay*	friendship
	moitié	*mwah-tay*	half
-tion	addition	*ah-dee-syohN*	addition
-ure	ceinture	*saN-tewr*	belt
	confiture	*kohN-fee-*	jam, jelly
	couverture	*tewr*	blanket
		koo-vehr-	
		tewr	

There are some logical categories that can help you recognize feminine nouns.

- Names of automobiles: *une Fiat, une Porsche, une Renault*

- Common names of businesses: *boulangerie* (bake shop), *charcuterie* (deli), *parfumerie* (perfume shop)

- Names of school subjects and sciences: *chimie* (chemistry), *médecine* (medical science), and those ending in *-graphie* like *géographie* and *photographie*

Recognizing Masculine Nouns

As with feminine nouns, word endings can also be used to identify a lot masculine nouns.

Noun Ending	Examples		
-acle	spectacle	*spehk-tahkl*	show
-age*	étage	*ay-tahzh*	floor (story)
	fromage	*froh-mahzh*	cheese

	maquillage	*mah-kee-yahzh*	makeup
-aire	anniversaire		birthday
	commentaire		commentary
-al	journal	*zhoor-nahl*	newspaper
	bocal	*boh-kahl*	jar
	animal	*ah-nee-mahl*	animal
-eau**	bateau	*bah-to*	boat
	chapeau	*sha-po*	hat
	couteau	*koo-to*	knife
-er and -ier	atelier	*ah-tuh-lyay*	studio
	escalier	*ehs-kah-lyay*	stairs
	papier	*pah-pyay*	paper
-et	billet	*bee-yeh*	ticket
	briquet	*bree-keh*	lighter
-isme	cyclisme	*see-kleez-muh*	
	capitalisme		capitalism
	tourisme		tourism
-ment	avertissemnet	*ah-vehr-tees-mahN*	warning
	changement	*shahNzh-mahN*	
	médicament	*may-dee-kah-mahN*	medicine

* except page *pahzh* (page); plage *plazh* (beach)
** except eau *o* (water); peau *po* (skin)

Most of the nouns in the following categories are masculine:

- Colors: le bleu (blue), le rouge (red), le vert (green)

- Languages: le chinois (Chinese), le français (French)

- Names of metals: acier (steel), fer (iron), or (gold)

- Metric units of measure: centimètre, kilo, mètre

- Names of trees: chêne (oak), olivier (olive), pommier (apple)

All the days of the week and months of the year are masculine. The seasons are also masculine.

winter	l'hiver	*lee-vehr*
spring	le printemps	*luh praN-than*
summer	l'été	*lay-tay*
fall / autumn	l'automme	*lo-tohn*

Gender Changes

A number of feminine nouns are derived from the masculine form. A simple and fast way to create these nouns is to add an *e* to their male counterpart. The resulting words differ in pronunciation. For the masculine, the final consonant is silent. For the feminine noun, the consonant must be pronounced due to the presence of an additional *e*. In cases where the masculine has a final nasal sound, the nasality is lost for the feminine ending.

Le (L'), Un		La (L'), Une		English
ami	*ah-mee*	amie	*ah-mee*	friend
avocat	*ah-vo-kah*	avocate	*ah-vo-kaht*	lawyer
client	*klee-yahN*	cliente	*klee-yahNt*	client
cousin	*koo-zaN*	cousine	*koo-zeen*	cousin

Some masculine noun endings have a corresponding feminine ending. These nouns are usually names of professions.

Ending	Masculine		English
-an	paysan	*peh-ee-zahN*	peasant
-anne	paysanne	*peh-ee-zahn*	

-er -ère	épicier *ay-pee-syay* épicière *ay-pee-syehr*	grocer
-eur -euse	programmeur *proh-grah-muhr* programmeuse *proh-grah-muhz*	programmer
-ien -ienne	pharmacien *fahr-mah-syaN* pharmacienne *fahr-mah-syehn*	pharmacist
-on -onne	patron *pah-trohN* patronne pah-trohn	boss
-teur -trice	acteur *ahk-tuhr* actrice *ahk-trees*	actor actress

Note: Names of professions are never followed by the article *un* or *une*.

Il est pharmacien.   Elle est programmeuse.

Not all feminine nouns are derived from masculine nouns. In these cases, you may need a dictionary to figure them out. Here are a few examples:

garçon	boy	fille	girl
homme	male	femme	female
roi	king	reine	queen
oncle	uncle	tante	aunt

Number

Just like in English, French nouns take a plural form when they refer to more than one person, place, object, or concept. Simply changing the noun isn't enough, though. The accompanying noun identifier should be made plural, too.

Noun Markers	Feminine	Masculine
the (definite)	les	les
some (indefinite)	des	des

As you can see, the plural form of these articles are the same for both feminine and masculine. Therefore, they can't be used to determine gender. They specify only that the speaker is talking about more than one noun.

Few Simple Rules

For most French nouns, forming the plural is as simple as adding an -s. Because the final s is silent, the pronunciation will stay the same. You'll only notice the difference in the identifier that precedes it.

la fille	*lah-fee-y*	les filles	*lay-fee-y*	girl(s)
un enfant	*uhN-nahN-fahN*	des enfants	*day-zahN-fahN*	child(ren)
le chat	*luh-sha*	les chats	*lay-sha*	cat(s)
une maison	*ewn-meh-zohN*	des maisons	*day-meh-zohN*	house(s)

When nouns end in *-eau* and *-eu*, add *x* instead of *s*. Here are some words you've already learned:

bateau	bateaux	boat(s)
chapeau	chapeaux	hat(s)
couteau	couteaux	knife/knives

- An exception to this is *le pneu* (tire): *le pneus*

For nouns ending in -al, drop the -al and add -aux.

cheval	chevaux	horse(s)
hôpital	hôpitaux	hospital(s)
signal	signal	signal(s)

- Three exceptions to this are le bal (ball): les bals; le carnaval (carnival): les carnavals; and le festival (festival): les festivals

Nouns ending in -ou generally take and s to form the plural. The following words are exceptions. They take an -x instead.

bijou	bijoux	bee-zhoo	jewel(s)
chou	choux	shoo	cabbage(s)
caillou	cailloux	kah-yoo	pebble(s)
genou	genoux	zhuh-noo	knee(s)
hibou	hiboux	ee-boo	owl(s)
joujou	joujoux	zhoo-zhoo	toy(s)

For singular nouns that end in s, x, or z, the plural form is just the same.

le prix	luh-pree	les prix	lay-pree	price(s), prize(s)
le fils	luh-fees	les fils	lay-fees	son(s)
le bras	luh-brah	les bras	lay-brah	arm(s)
la mois	lah-mwah	les mois	lay-mwah	month(s)
le repas	luh-ruh-pah	les repas	lay-ruh-pah	meal(s)
la croix	lah-krwah	les croix	lay-croix	crosses
la voix	lah-vwah	les vwah	lay-vwah	voice(s)

In English, we have some words that are always plural. The French also have their own. Here are some nouns that you may find useful:

les ciseaux *m.*	*lay-see-zo*	scissors
les lunettes *f.*	*lay-lew-neht*	eyeglasses
les gens *m.*	*lay-zhahN*	people
les vacances *f.*	*lay-vah-kahNs*	vacation
les cheveux *m.*	*lay-shuh-vuh*	hair

Note: In English, some words never take a plural form. A couple of examples are vacation and hair. In contrast, as you can see from the previous table, the French for vacation and hair are always in the plural form.

More On Articles

Now that you're acquainted with the French articles, which accompany the nouns most of the time, let's take a deeper look into them.

Definite Articles

The French has three forms of the definite article "the": *le, la,* and *les.* Remember that *le* and *la* are shortened to *l'* when followed by a noun that starts with a vowel or *h.*

Use definite articles in these cases when "the" is skipped in English:

- When you're stating a preference or negative preference

    J'aime les bananes. (I like bananas.)
    Tu n'aimes pas le chocolat. (You don't like chocolate.)

- When naming a category in general, such as *les femmes, le pain* (bread), and *l'amour* (love)

42

C'est la vie. (That's life.)

- When naming a geographical place or language

    le Japon (Japan)
    Il apprend le français. (He's learning French.)

- Before a certain day when you want to express "every"

    le mardi (every Tuesday)
    le samedi (on Saturdays)

- Instead of a possessive adjective, when referring to a body part with a reflexive verb.

    Nous nous lavons les pieds. (We wash our feet.)

Indefinite Articles

There are four forms of indefinite articles in French: *un, une, des,* and *de.* You're already familiar with the first three, which were introduced in the earlier sections of this chapter. Use them the way you use their English equivalent.

De (*d'* when followed by a noun starting with a vowel or a silent -*h*) is only used with a negative verb. Here are some examples:

Il ne veut pas d'enfants. (He doesn't want any children.)
Je n'ai pas de monnaie. (I don't have any change.)

Note: When the negative verb is *être* (to be), don't use *de.* Treat the sentence as if it was affirmative.

Partitive Articles

Use partitive articles to indicate part of a whole, or an indefinite quantity that's equivalent to *some* or *any.*

Article	Usage	Example
du (de + le)	before a singular masculine noun that starts w/ a consonant	du pain (some bread)
de la	before a singular feminine noun that starts w/ a consonant	de la soupe (some soup)
de l'	before any singular noun that begins with a vowel	de l'eau (some water)
des (de + les)	before any plural noun	de petits pois (some/any peas)
de	before any noun after a negative verb	pas de café (no/not any coffe)

Partitive articles are used in the following ways:

- When a noun describes a partial category

  Nous buvons de l'eau minerale. (We drink some bottled water.)
  Il met du sucre dans son thé. (He puts (some) sugar in his tea.)

- After the verb *faire* (to practice/do/make) + a sport, school subject, or a musical instrument

  Mark fait de l'escrime. (Mark fences.)
  Il fait du piano. (He plays the piano.)
  Il fait de la chemie. (He studies chemistry.)

Note:

- When an adjective precedes a plural noun, use *de* even when the sentence isn't negative.

Il prepare de bons desserts. (He prepares good deserts.)

- In English, *some* or *any* may be omitted but their counterpart must always be used in French. They must also be placed before each noun.

  Apportez-moi de la mousse et du café. (Bring me some mousse and (some) coffee.)

Choosing the Correct Article

If you're feeling confused about which article to use, here are a few tips on how to pick the right one.

Partitive vs. Definite

A partitive article refers to a partial category. A definite article is used to denote a whole category. If you drink beer, you only drink some (requires a partitive article) and not all the beer there is in the planet. If you say money is necessary, you're talking about money in general or as a whole category.

  Partitive: *Quand on travaille, on gagne **de** l'argent.* (When you work, you make money.)
  Definite: ***L'argent** est necessaire.* (Money is necessary.)

Partitive vs. Indefinite

Use partitive articles for something that you can't really count such as water *de l'eau* (water) and *du café* (coffee). For something that you can count such as *un chiene* (dog) and *une tasse* (cup), use indefinite articles.

  Partitive (uncountable): *Il veut **du** café.* (He wants some coffee.)

45

Indefinite (countable): *Il veut **une** pommes.* (He wants an apple.)

Chapter 5: Verbs

Verbs signify a state of being or an action. To form a sentence, a verb requires a subject, which is directly expressed in a statement. In a command, the subject can be implied.

Subject Pronouns

Just like in English, the subject can be a noun or a pronoun and is given a number and a person. You're already familiar with a number of nouns. It's time to get acquainted with the French subject pronouns that you'll need to conjugate verbs.

Singular			Plural		
je	*zhuh*	I	nous	noo	we
tu	*tew*	you	vous	*voo*	you
il	*eel*	he, it	ils	*eel*	they
elle	*ehl*	she, it	elles	*ehl*	they
on	*ohN*	one, we			

Note:

- *Je* becomes j' in front of a word that begins with a vowel. Unlike the English *I,* it's not written in uppercase unless a sentence starts with it.

- Use *tu* when talking to a single person you're familiar with, such as a friend, family, or a child. Don't say *tu* to a person you should be respectful to, someone you've never met before, or a business relation.

- *Vous* is the plural for *tu.* It's also the formal or polite form of *you,* both singular and plural. Just like in English, it always requires the plural form of verb even when used to address a single person.

- *Il* is used to refer to a masculine noun or thing. In addition, use *il* in phrases that can only be expressed in an impersonal mode, for instance *il faut* (it's necessary). *Il* is also used in all expressions regarding weather and time.

- *Ils* and *elles* mean *they*. Use *ils* when referring to an all-masculine group or a mix of masculine and feminine subjects. As long as there's one masculine subject in the group described, use *ils*. *Elles* is strictly for an all-feminine group.

- Use *on* when referring to people in general. *On* can also mean *one* or *someone* but it can never refer to a thing. When used as the informal equivalent of *nous,* it still takes a third person singular verb.

Regular vs. Irregular Verbs

Verbs exist in many forms. Infinitive refers to the form before a verb has been conjugated. Think of an infinitive as a verb in which no one performs the action.

Conjugation is the changing of the ending of a verb so that it agrees with the subject and the tense or time frame. In our native language, we conjugate all of the time. It comes naturally that we don't even need to take note of what we're doing.

In English, verbs in their infinitive form follows the word *to*: to swim, to run, to fly. In French, infinitives end in either *-er, -ir,* or *-re*.

There are two types of verbs: regular and irregular. They're categorized based on how they are conjugated. For the regular verbs, each family follows a pattern of rules so when you learn those rules, conjugation will be easy. Unfortunately, there are no rules for irregular verbs so you'll have to memorize all of their forms.

Present Tense

You use the present tense of a verb in French when you need to express what is happening now or what happens in the present in general. You also use it to ask for instructions or imply the immediate future.

To conjugate regular verbs in the present tense, just drop the ending (*-er*, *-ir*, or *-re*) and add the ending that agrees with the subject.

-er Verbs

The good news for you is that the *-er* family includes at least 80% of French verbs. Once you get to learn their pattern of conjugation by heart, you'll be able to conjugate a huge chunk of French verbs.

The following table shows you how regular *-er* verbs are conjugated.

Subject	parler (to speak)
je	parl**e**
tu	parl**es**
il, elle, on	parl**e**
nous	parl**ons**
vous	parl**ez**
ils, elles	parl**ent**

Here are some of the most common regular -er verbs that you'll use in any given situation:

French	Pronunciation	English
aider	*eh-day*	to help
aimer	*eh-may*	to like, love
chercher	*shehr-say*	to look for
commencer	*koh-mahN-say*	to begin
demander	*duh-mahN-day*	to ask
dépenser	*day-puhN-say*	to spend (money)
donner	*doh-nay*	to give
écouter	*ay-koo-tay*	to listen (to)
étudier	*ay-tew-dyay*	to study
fermer	*fehr-may*	to close
habiter	*ah-bee-tay*	to live (in)
jouer	*zhoo-ay*	to play
oublier	*oo-blee-yay*	to forget
manger	*mahN-zhay*	to eat
penser	*pahN-say*	to think
préparer	*pray-pah-ray*	to prepare
présenter	*pray-zahN-tay*	to present, introduce
regarder	*ruh-gahr-day*	to look (at), to watch
rencontrer	*rahN-kohN-tray*	to meet
signer	*see-nyay*	to sign
téléphoner	*tay-lay-foh-nay*	to telephone
travailler	*trah-vah-yay*	to work
trouver	*troo-vay*	to find
voyager	*vwah-yah-zhay*	to travel

Note:

50

- For verbs ending in -*cer,* change *c* to *ç* before adding -*ons* corresponding to the pronoun *nous* in order to retain the soft sound.

annoncer	nous annonçons	we announce
commencer	nous commençons	we begin
prononcer	nous prononçons	we pronounce
remplacer	nous remplaçons	we replace

- For verbs ending in -*ger,* keep the soft *g* sound by only dropping the final *r* and keeping the *e* before adding -*ons.*

changer	nous changeons	we change
manger	nous mangeons	we eat
nager	nous nageons	we swim
voyager	nous voyageon	we travel

- For verbs ending in -*yer,* retain the *y* for *nous* and *vous.* Replace it with *i* for all others. This change is optional for verbs ending in -*ayer* such as *payer* (to pay [for]).

	employer (to use)	envoyer (to send)	nettoyer (to send)
je	emploie	envoie	nettoie
tu	emploies	envoies	nettoies
il, elle, on	imploie	envoie	nettoie
nous	employons	envoyons	nettoyons
vous	employez	envoyez	nettoyez
ils, elles	emploient	envoient	nettoient

- For verbs with *e/é* +a consonant before ending in -*er,* replace *e/é* with *è* in all forms except for *nous* and *vous.*

51

	acheter (to buy)	préférer (to prefer)
je	achète	préfère
tu	achètes	préfères
il, elle, on	achète	préfère
nous	achetons	préférons
vous	achetez	préférez
ils, elles	achètent	préfèrent

- For the words *appeler* (to call) and *jeter* (to throw away), double the consonant that comes before *-er* in all forms except *nous* and *vous*. Note that only a few verbs follow this pattern of conjugation.

	appeler (to call)	jeter (to throw away)
je	appelle	jette
tu	appelles	jettes
il, elle, on	appelle	jette
nous	appelons	jetons
vous	appelez	jetez
ils, elles	appellent	jettent

-ir Verbs

The second most common type of French verb is the *-ir* family. The following table shows you how regular *-ir* verbs are conjugated.

Subject	choisir (to choose)
je	choisis
tu	choisis
il, elle, on	choisit
nous	choisissons
vous	choisissez
ils, elles	choisissent

And here are some regular -*ir* verbs that will be useful to you.

French	Pronunciation	English
finir	*fee-neer*	to finish
guérir	*gay-reer*	to cure
jouir	*zhoo-eer*	to enjoy
réfléchir	*ray-flay-sheer*	to reflect, think
réussir	*ray-ew-seer*	to succeed

A fairly large chunk (about 30 verbs) of the -*ir* family don't follow the conjugation pattern and are considered irregular verbs. For some of these verbs, the easiest way of conjugating is to separate the singular from the plural form. For the plural forms, drop -*ir* while for the singular, include the adjacent consonant before adding the corresponding endings.

	dormir (to sleep)	partir (to leave)
je	dor**s**	par**s**
tu	dor**s**	par**s**
il, elle, on	dor**t**	par**t**
nous	dorm**ons**	part**ons**
vous	dorm**ez**	part**ez**
ils, elles	dorm**ent**	part**ent**

Here are some more common words that are included in this sub-group.

French	Pronunciation	English
mentir	*mahN-teer*	to (tell a) lie
sentir	*sahN-teer*	to feel, to smell
servir	*sehr-veer*	to serve
sortir	*sohr-teer*	to go out, to exit

Note:

- A few -*ir* verbs act as if they're regular -*ir* verbs. To conjugate, drop the -*ir* and add the corresponding ending for the -*er* verb. Verbs of this type include *découvrir* (to discover), *offrir* (to offer), *ouvrir* (to open), and *souffrir* (to suffer).

- *Tenir* (to have) and *venir* (to come) a part of a special group of verbs along with their siblings – compound verbs form with a prefix + *tenir/venir*. Included in this group are *appartenir* (to belong), *devenir* (to become), *revenir* (to come back), *se souvenir* (to remember), and *soutenir* (to support). The following demonstrates how words in this group are conjugated.

Subject	tenir (to have)	venir (to come)
je	tiens	viens
tu	tiens	viens
il, elle, on	tient	vient
nous	tenons	venons
vous	tenez	venez
ils, elles	tiennent	viennent

- For *voir* (to see), the *nous* and *vous* forms are much like that of the -*yer* verbs. One common irregular -*re* verb follows the same pattern.

Subject	voir (to see)	croire (to believe)
je	vois	crois
tu	vois	crois
il, elle, on	voit	croit
nous	voyons	croyons
vous	voyez	croyez

ils, elles	voient	croient

-re Verbs

The third and final groups of verbs is the -re family. The following shows how they are conjugated:

Subject	vendre (to sell)
je	vend**s**
tu	vend**s**
il, elle, on	vend
nous	vend**ons**
vous	vend**ez**
ils, elles	vend**ent**

And here are some -re verbs that you will commonly use.

French	Pronunciation	English
attendre	*ah-tahNdr*	to wait (for)
descendre	*deh-sahNdr*	to go (come) down
entendre	*ahN-tahNdr*	to hear
perdre	*pehrdr*	to lose
répondre	*ray-pohNdr*	to answer

Note:

- For the verb *prendre* (to take) and other words derived from it such as *apprendre* (to learn) and *comprendre* (to understand), conjugation only follows the pattern for the singular forms. For the plural forms, the rules are different. *D* is dropped together with *re* and for the third person, the consonant is doubled.

Subject	prendre (to take)	apprendre (to learn)	comprendre (to understand)
je	prends	j'apprends	comprends

55

tu	prends	apprends	comprends
il, elle, on	prends	apprend	comprend
nous	prenons	apprenons	comprenons
vous	prenez	apprenez	comprenez
ils, elles	prennent	apprennent	comprennent

- The words *conduire* (to drive), *dire* (to say/tell), and *lire* (to read) follow another pattern which is similar to that of the sub-group of the *-ir* verbs. However, the *vous* form of *dire* diverts from this pattern.

Subject	conduire (to drive)	dire (to say/tell)	lire (to read)
je	conduis	dis	lis
tu	conduit	dis	lis
il, elle, on	conduit	dit	lit
nous	conduisons	disons	lisons
vous	conduisez	dites	lisez
ils, elles	consduisent	disent	lisent

- *Écrire* (to write) and *mettre* (to put) behave much like *conduire*. The difference is in the formation of their plural counterpart.

Subject	écrire (to write)	mettre (to put)
je	**j'ecris**	mets
tu	écris	mets
il, elle, on	écrit	met
nous	écrivons	mettons
vous	écrivez	mettez
ils, elles	écrivent	mettent

More Irregular Verbs

In English, the most commonly used verbs - and their different conjugations – are *to be, to do, to go,* and *to have.* The same is true in the French language. The table that follows shows you the conjugation of these four words in the present tense.

	être (to be)	faire (to do)	aller (to go)	avoir (to have)
je	suis	fais	vais	**j'ai**
tu	es	fais	vas	as
il, elle, on	est	fait	va	a
nous	sommes	faisons	allons	avons
vous	êtes	faites	allez	avez
ils, elles	sont	font	vont	ont

The verbs *devoir* (must/to have to), *pouvoir* (can/to be able to) and *vouloir* (to want) are quite significant because they act as helper verbs to another verb. When used as a helper verb, it is conjugated but the other verb remains in infinitive, unless you're dealing with a past tense.

	devoir (must)	pouvoir (can)	vouloir (to want)
je	dois	peux	veux
tu	dois	peux	veux
il, elle, on	doit	peut	veut
nous	devons	pouvons	voulons
vous	devez	pouvez	voulez
ils, elles	doivent	peuvent	veulent

Note: *Boire* (to drink) is conjugated the same way as *devoir.*

The Past

To express an action or event that occurred and was begun or completed at a definite time in the past, the French use the *passé compose* or compound past. The compound past is made up of two parts: the auxiliary or helping verb conjugated in its present-tense form and the past participle of another verb.

In most instances, the helping verb used is *avoir* (to have). *Être* (to be) is generally used with verbs showing action that denotes a change. The action that actually took place is expressed by the past participle.

Regular Verbs

Forming the past participle of French verbs is quite easy. Drop the ending and then add the corresponding letter depending on which group the verb belongs to.

-er verbs	*-ir* verbs	*-re* verbs
travailler	réussir	entendre
travaill**é**	réuss**i**	entend**u**

Elle a travaillé en France.	She studied in France.
Nous avons réussi.	We succeeded.
J'ai entendu une chanson.	I heard a song.

Irregular Verbs

Unfortunately, you can't rely on the three types of verbs to determine how an irregular verb forms its past participle. In most cases, they can be grouped according to their endings but you will really need to memorize them.

• Past participles ending in *-is*:

Infinitive	Past Participle	English (Past Participle)
apprendre	appris	learned
comprendre	compris	understood
metter	mis	put (on)
prendre	pris	taken

• Past participles ending in -*it*:

Infinitive	Past Participle	English (Past Participle)
conduire	conduit	driven
dire	dit	said, told
écrire	écrit	written

• Past participles in -*u*:

Infinitive	Past Participle	English (Past Participle)
avoir	eu	had
boire	bu	drunk
connaître	connu	known
croire	cru	believed
devoir	dû	had to, owed
lire	lu	read
plaire	plu	pleased
pleuvoir	plu	rained
pouvoir	pu	had been able to
recevoir	reçu	received
savoir	su	know
tenir	tenu	held
venir	venu	come
voir	vu	seen
vouloir	voulu	wanted

• Other irregular past participles:

Infinitive	Past Participle	English (Past Participle)
être	été	been
faire	fait	made, done
mourir	mort	died
naître	né	been born
offrir	offert	offered
ouvrir	ouvert	opened

Note that when a verb contains a smaller verb, their past participles are generally formed in the same manner.

mettre	mis	ouvrir	ouvert
promettre	promis	découvrir	découvert

Être vs Avoir

Not a lot of common verbs take *étre* as an auxiliary to form the *passé compose*. There's a mnemonic that you can use to remember these verbs: DR & MRS VANDERTRAMPP. The asterisk that comes after the past participle denotes an irregular verb.

Infinitive	Past Participle	English (Infinitive)
Devenir	devenu *	to become
Revenir	revenu *	to return
Mourir	mort *	to die
Retourner	retourné	to return
Sortir	sorti	to go out
Venir	venu *	to come
Arriver	arrivé	to arrive
Naître	né *	to be born

Descendre	descendu	to go down
Entrer	entré	to enter
Rentrer	rentré	to return
Tomber	tombé	to fall
Rester	resté	to remain
Aller	allé	to go
Monter	monté	to go up
Passer	passé	to pass by
Partir	parti	to leave

When *avoir* is the auxiliary verb, the past participle generally stays the same. Only the auxiliary is required to agree with the subject.

Elle a **ouvert** la porte.	She opened the door.
Nous avons **ouvert** les fenêtres.	We opened the windows.

In the case of *étre,* the past participle must also agree in number and gender with the subjects.

Feminine Subjects	Masculine Subjects	English
Je suis venu**e**.	Je suis venu.	I arrived.
Tu es venu**e**.	Tu es venu.	You arrived.
Vous êtes venu**e**.	Vous êtes venu.	You arrived. (singular)
Elle est venu**e**.	Il est venu	She/he arrived.
Nous sommes venu**es**.	Nous sommes venu**s**.	We arrived.
Vous êtes venu**es**.	Vous êtes venu**s**.	You arrived. (plural)
Elles sont venu**es**.	Ils sont venu**s**.	They arrived.

Here are the proper uses of the compound past:

- Relating an event or occurrence in the past that has completely ended

Il est allé en France il y a trois ans.	He went to France three years ago.
Nous avons mangé des pommes hier.	We ate apples yesterday.

- Listing actions that happened one after another

D'abord il a marché, puis il a couru, et il a nagé.	First he walked, then he ran, and he swam.
Nous avons mange; puis nous avons dormi.	We ate; then we slept.

- Expressing an event or action that was repeated a specified number of times

J'ai vu ce film deux fois.	I saw that movie twice.

The Imperfect

The *imparfait* is used to describe repeated or continuous events, actions, states, or situations in the past. To conjugate the imperfect, drop the -*ons* from the *nous* form in the present tense then add these endings:

je	-ais	nous	-ions
tu	-ais	vous	-iez
il	-ait	ils	-aient

Only *être* follows a different pattern.

j'étais	nous étions
tu étais	vous étiez
il était	ils étaient

Here are the proper uses of the imperfect:

- Describing what was in the past or what used to happen repeatedly

Il écoutait une chanson.	He was listening to a song.
Elle venait ici le dimanche.	She used to come here on Saturdays.

- Describing people, time, or objects in the past

Nous étions très heureux.	We were very happy
C'était le matin.	It was morning.
Le poisson était frais.	The fish was fresh.

- Expressing a state of mind in the past

Je croyais en toi.	I believed in you.
Tu voulais aller en Allemagne.	You wanted to go to Germany.

- Describing a condition taking place when another action happened

Il pleuvait quand ils sont sortis.	It was raining when they went out.
J'étudiais quand il est arrive.	I was studying when he arrived.

The Future

Forming the future tense of most regular verbs is quite easy. For -er and -ir verbs, just add the following endings to the infinitive to form the simple future. For the *-re* family, drop the final *e* before adding these suffixes. Note that there's no French equivalent to the English word *will*.

je	-ai	nous	-ons
tu	-as	vous	-ez
il, elle	-a	ils, elles	-ont

Je dormirai.	I will sleep.
Ils joueront demain.	They will play tomorrow.
Il vendra sa voiture.	He will sell his car.

Note:

- For verbs ending in *-yer* (such as *employer*), replace *y* with *i* before adding the future ending. For those ending in *-ayer,* this change is optional. Both spellings are accepted.

- For *jeter* and *appeler,* double the consonant that precedes --er before adding the future endings.

Irregular Verbs

A number of irregular verbs behave rather unusually in the future tense. They use a completely different stem. To conjugate, add the future ending to the stems showed in the following:

Infinitive	English	Future-Tense Stem
aller	to go	ir-
avoir	to have	aur-
courir	to run	courr-
devour	to have to, to owe	devr-
envoyer	to send	enverr-

être	to be	ser-
faire	to do	fer-
falloir	to be necessary	faudr
mourir	to die	mourr-
pleuvoir	to rain	pleuvr-
recevoir	to receive	recevr-
savoir	to know	saur-
tenir	to hold	tiendr-
venir	to come	viendr-
voir	to see	verr-
vouloir	to want	voudr-

Other Ways of Expressing the Future

Like in English, there are other ways to talk about the future aside from using the simple future tense. You can use the present to indicate the future by adding expression of time. The following is a list of common French time expressions used with the future tense. Note that you can use either the present or future tenses with these expressions.

Expression	English
après	after
bientôt	soon
ensuite / puis	then/next
plus tard	later
tout à l'heure	in a little bit
dans + [amount of time]	in + [amount of time]
ce soir	tonight / this evening
cet après-midi	this afternoon
demain	tomorrow
demain matin	tomorrow morning
demian après midi	tomorrow afternoon

65

demain soir	tomorrow night / evening
après-demain	the day after tomorrow
[day of the week] + prochain	next + [day of the week]
la semaine prochaine	next week
le mois prochain	next month
le weekend prochain	next weekend
l'année prochaine	next year
un jour	one day

Je te vois demain.	I'll see you tomorrow.
Nous visitons la France le mois prochain.	We will visit France next month.
Il commence lundi prochain.	He will start next Monday.

Another way to talk about the future is by conjugating the word *aller* (to go) in the present tense and combining it with the infinitive of the actual verb expressing the action.

Ils vont courir.	They're going to run.
Nous allons avoir un bébé.	We're going to have a baby.
Je vais dormir.	I'm going to sleep.

The Conditional

The conditional expresses what would happen or what the subject would do under certain situations. It is formed by adding the imperfect ending to the stems of future tense of all verbs.

je	-ais	nous	-ions
tu	-ais	vous	-iez
il	-ait	ils	-aient

This form is used to describe a hypothetical event, to politely express or offer an advice, to express wishes, and to state a future event from a past context.

Si j'avais un million de dollars, je ferais le tour du monde.	If I had a million dollars, I would travel the world.
Tu devrais manger plus de légumes.	You should eat more vegetables.
Pourriez-vous venir me chercher plus tard?	Could you pick me up later?
Voudrais-tu de l'aide?	Would you like some help?
Ils ont dit qu'ils allaient nettoyer la maison.	They said they would clean the house.

Make no Mistake

Indeed, it will take some time before you can master the rules of conjugation for regular verbs, let alone memorize the different forms of the irregular ones. But there are some very common mistakes that you're likely to commit. Here are three of those mistakes.

1. Using different verbs to refer to means of transportation

When verbs such as *to walk, to drive, to fly,* and *to swim* are used to talk about means of transportations, don't translate them directly into French. When you want to say you drove or walked to some place, use the combination of *aller* + à or *en* + means of transportation.

English	French	Literal Translation
to walk	aller à pied	to go by foot
to swim	aller à la nage	to go by swimming
to drive	aller à voiture	to go in a car
to fly	aller en avion	to go in a plane

yada

Les enfants vont à pied à l'école.	The children walk to school.
Ils vont en voiture à la campagne tous les samedis.	They drive to the countryside every Saturday.
Il est allé dans un avion pour Paris la nuit dernière.	He flew to Paris last night.

2. Making your own *-ing* form of the verb

While in English the present tense can be expressed using two verb forms, there's only one form in French – the simple tense. When you want to express something that is happening right at this moment, never put the conjugated form of *être* between the subject and the verb.

Wrong: Il est étudie. **Correct**: Il étudie.	He is studying.

3. Using *être* instead of *avoir*

In English, we use the conjugated form of *to be* when expressing certain conditions that we experience such as hunger. In French, they use *avoir* instead of *être*.

J'ai faim.	I'm hungry.
J'ai soif.	I'm thirsty.
J'ai peur.	I'm scared.
J'ai chaud.	I'm warm.
J'ai froid.	I'm cold.

Although not limited to verbs, another mistake that you may easily fall into is being tricked by false cognates. A cognate is a word that is spelled exactly or almost the same as an English word and that has the same meaning, such as animal and table. Here's a list of some common false cognates that you should watch out for.

English Word	French Cognate	French Meaning
actually	actuellement	currently
to assist	assister	to attend
to attend	attendre	to wait for
comment	comment	how
a demand	une demande	a request
deception	déception	disappointment
entrée	entrée	appetizer / starter
eventually	éventuellement	possibly
gross	gros(se)	fat
library	librairie	bookstore
location	location	rental
to pass (an exam)	passer (un examen)	to take an exam
patron	patron	boss
to rest	rester	to stay
rude	rude	harsh

sale	sale	dirty
to travel	travailler	to work

Chapter 6: Adjectives

Adjectives are used to describe nouns. While you can form a proper sentence with just a noun/pronoun and a verb, you can give it more color and change the context with adjectives.

In French, adjectives must agree with the gender and number of the nouns they modify. If the subject is feminine plural, the adjective must also be feminine plural. If the subject is masculine singular, then the adjective must be masculine singular. In other words, all words in a sentence must agree with each other.

Forming Feminine Adjectives

The default form of French adjectives is masculine singular. You can easily make it feminine by adding an -e. Note that adding -e changes the word's pronunciation. The silent final consonant in the masculine form is pronounced in the feminine form.

Masculine/Feminine	Pronunciation	English
âgé(e)	*ah-zyay*	aged, old
américain(e)	*ah-may-ree-kahN/kehn*	American
amusant(e)	*ah-mew-zahN(t)*	amusing, fun
blond(e)	*blohN(d)*	blond
charmant(e)	*shahr-mahN(t)*	charming
content(e)	*kohN-tahN(t)*	glad
élégant(e)	*ay-lay-gahN(t)*	elegant
fort(e)	*fohr(t)*	strong
français(e)	*frahN-seh(z)*	French
grand(e)	*grahN(d)*	big

intellingent(e)	*aN-teh-lee-zhahN(t)*	intelligent
joli(e)	*zhoh-lee*	pretty
petit(e)	*puh-tee(t)*	small
poli(e)	*poh-lee*	polite

Some masculine adjectives already end in *e*. For these words, you don't need to make any changes. The spelling and pronunciation for both the feminine and masculine are the same.

Masculine/Feminine	Pronunciation	English
célèbre	*say-lehbr*	famous
comique	*koh-meek*	comical
facile	*fah-seel*	easy
honnête	*oh-neht*	honest
mince	*maNs*	thin
proper	*prohpr*	clean
sale	*sahl*	dirty
triste	*treest*	sad

Note:

- For masculine adjectives ending in -*eux*, drop *x* and add -*se*. This gives the ending of the feminine a *z* sound.

Masculine	Feminine	Pronunciation
affectueux	affectueuse	*ah-feh-tew-uh(z)*
ambitieux	ambitieuse	*ahN-bee-syuh(z)*
délicieux	délicieuse	*day-lee-syuh(z)*
généreux	généreuse	*zhay-nay-ruh(z)*
heureux (happy)	heureuse	*uh-ruh(z)*
sérieux	sérieuse	*say-ryuh(z)*

- For masculine adjectives ending in -f, drop f and add -ve to form the feminine.

Masculine	Feminine	Pronunciation
actif	active	*ahk-teef/teev*
attentif	attentive	*ah-tahN-teef/teev*
imaginatif	imaginative	*ee-mah-zhee-nah-teef/teev*
naïf	naïve	*nah-eef/eev*
sportif (athletic)	sportive	*spohr-teef/teev*

- For masculine adjectives ending in -er, change *er to ère.*

Masculine	Feminine	Pronunciation	English
cher	chère	*shehr*	dear, expensive
dernier	dernière	*dehr-nyay/nyehr*	last
étranger	étrangère	*ay-trahN-zhay/zhehr*	foreign
fier	fière	*fyehr*	proud
premier	première	*pruh-myay/myehr*	first

- For some masculine adjectives, you need to double the final consonant before adding an -e to form the femine.

Masculine	Feminine	Pronunciation	English
ancien	ancienne	*ahN-syaN/syehn*	ancient, old
bas	basse	*bah(s)*	low
bon	bonne	*bohN/bohn*	good
européen	européenne	*ew-roh-pay-aN/ehn*	European
gentil	gentile	*zhahN-tee-y*	nice, kind
gros	grosse	*gro(s)*	fat, big
mignon	mignonne	*mee-nyohN/nyohn*	cute

- For some masculine adjectives, the feminine form is quite irregular so you need to memorize each one of them.

Masculine	Feminine	Pronunciation	English
beau *	belle	*bo/belle*	beautiful
blanc	blanche	*blahN/blahNsh*	white
complet	complète	*kohN-pleh(t)*	complete
doux	douce	*doo(s)*	sweet, gentle
faux	fausse	*fo(s)*	false
favori	favorite	*fah-voh-ree(t)*	favorite
frais	fraiche	*freh(sh)*	fresh
long	longue	*lohN(g)*	long
nouveau *	nouvelle	*noo-vo/vehl*	new
vieux *	vieille	*vyuh/vyay*	old

* These adjectives have two masculine singular forms. When followed by a noun that starts with a vowel sound, the adjectives are *bel, nouvel, and vieil.*

Forming Plural Adjectives

In most cases, plural adjectives are formed by adding -*s* to the feminine singular or masculine singular form. The -*s* is silent so the pronunciation of the word does not change.

Masculine S.	Masculine P.	Feminine S.	Feminine P.
bleu	bleus	bleue	bleues
charmant	charmants	charmante	charmantes
content	contents	contente	contentes
dur	durs	dure	dures
joli	jolis	jolie	jolies

Note:

- For adjectives ending in -*s* or -*x*, you don't need to add the -*s*. A few examples are *gris* (gray), *heureux* (happy), *amoureux* (in love), and *jaloux* (jealous).

- For most masculine singular adjectives ending in -*al*, drop -*al* and add -*aux*. A few examples are *global/globaux*, *normal/normaux*, and *special/speciaux*. Exceptions to this are *fatal/fatals*, *final/finals*, *glacial/glacials*, and *naval/navals*.

- There are no irregular feminine plural endings.

Proper Placing of Adjectives

Unlike in English, French adjectives are generally placed after the noun they modify. Some are placed before the noun and still others can be placed either before or after.

une femme **intéressante**	an interesting woman
une fleur **jaune**	a yellow flower
une langue **étrangère**	a foreign language

Adjectives That Go Before Nouns

A group of adjectives referring to certain qualities must come before the noun they describe. To easily remember these adjectives, remember BAGS.

Beauty: *beau* (beautiful), *joli* (pretty)
Age: *jeune* (young), *nouveau* (new), *vieux* (old)
Goodness (or absence of it): *bon* (good), *gentil* (kind), *mauvais* (bad), *meilleur* (better)
Size: *gros* (fat), *haut* (high), *petit* (small)

Note: Some of the adjectives contained in the BAGS should be placed after the noun. These are: *laid* (ugly), *affreux* (atrocious), *âge* (old), and *méchant* (mean)

un appartement **laide**	an ugly apartment
des personnes **âgées**	old people
un **mauvaise** habitude	a bad habit
les **hautes** montagnes	the high mountains

Adjectives describing the order in which things come appear before nouns.

les **deuxième** enfant	the second child
la **première** semaine du mois	the first week of the month
le **seizième** siècle	the sixteenth century

The adjectives *autre* (other), *faux* (false), *méme* (same), and *tel* (such) are placed before nouns. When you use the word *tout* (all, every), you must place it not just before the noun but also before the article.

l'**autre** sans	the other meaning
un **faux** espoir	false hope
les **mêmes** vêtements	the same clothes
tous les matins	all mornings

Some adjectives can be placed before or after a noun. Their meanings depend on where they are placed. When placed before a noun, the meaning is more figurative while after, the meaning is quite literal.

Adjective	Before Noun	After Noun
ancient	former	antique, old
certain	some	sure

cher	dear	expensive
dernier	final	previous/last (time expression)
grand (people)	great	tall
pauvre	wretched, miserable	poor, broke
propre	own	clean
seul	only	alone
simple	mere	simple

Je veux une maison **propre**.	I want a **clean** house.
Je veux ma **propre** maison.	I want my **own** house.
J'ai donné à mon **cher** ami un cadeau **cher**.	I gave my **dear** friend an **expensive** gift.

Possessive Adjectives

To show possession, you can use the adjectives *my, your, her,* and so on. Possessive adjectives are places before the noun.

	For Masculine Singular Nouns	For Feminine Singular Nouns	For All Plural Nouns
my	mon (*mohN*)	ma (*mah*)	mes (*may*)
your (fam.)	ton (*tohN*)	ta (*tah*)	tes (*tey*)
his, her	son (*sohN*)	sa (*sah*)	ses (*ses*)
our	notre (*nohtr*)	notre (*nohtr*)	nos (*no*)
your (pol.)	votre (*vohtr*)	votre (*vohtr*)	vos (*vo*)
their	leur (*luhr*)	leur (*luhr*)	leurs (*luhr*)

Note: When *ma, ta,* and *sa* are followed by a noun beginning with a vowel or a silent *h*, they change to *mon, ton,* and *son,* respectively. This happens for pronunciation's sake.

Unlike in English, French possessive adjectives must agree in number and gender with the noun possessed and not with the possessor.

Il aime **ses** yeux.	He likes her eyes.
Elle aime **son** frère.	She loves her brother.
Il aime **son** frère.	He loves his brother.
Elle aime **sa** soeur.	She loves her sister.
Il aime **sa** soeur.	He loves his sister.

In the first example, the possessor is singular but the possessed noun is plural so the plural form of the adjective is used. *Son* is used in the second and third examples because *frère* is masculine. And finally, *sa* is used in the last two examples because *soeur* is feminine.

Demonstrative Adjectives

The demonstrative adjectives in English are *this, that, these,* and *those.* French has three demonstrative adjectives for singular and one in plural. They are placed before the noun they modify and must agree with them in gender and number.

- For masculine singular nouns starting with a consonant: **ce** *(suh)*

- For masculine singular nouns starting with a vowel: **cet** *(seht)*

- For all feminine nouns: **cette** *(seht)*

- For all plural nouns: **ces** *(ces)*

78

Note that if you use these adjectives, you won't be able to differentiate between *this* and *that* and between *these* and *those*. In order to do that, the French use compound demonstratives. *-ci* or *-la* is hyphenated to the noun. Add *-ci* if you mean *this* or *these*. Add *-la* for the others.

Je veux ce livre-ci mais pas ce livre-la.	I want this book but not that book.
J'aime ces lunettes-ci mais pas ces lunettes-la.	I like these glasses but not those glasses.

Making Comparisons

There are times when you need to compare people or things in order to give a more specific description. The common way of doing this in English is adding *-er* and *-est* to the adjective. These forms, however, do not exist in the French language.

Comparatives

Comparatives are used to compare two elements. There are three basic types of comparatives in French.

plus/que	more/than
moins/que	less/than
aussi/que	as/as

The first word is always followed by the adjective and *que*, which means *than*, is followed by the element you're comparing against. When que is followed by a word that starts with a vowel or a silent *h*, it become *qu'*.

Il est **plus** grand **que** son père.	He is taller than his father.
Ce sont **moins** chers **que** vos chaussures.	These are less expensive than your shoes.
L'arbre est **aussi** haut **qu'**un bâtiment de quatre étages.	The tree is as high as a four-story building.

Note:

- Just like in English, you don't say *plus bon* (more good) in French. The word for better is *meilleur* and since an adjective has to agree with the gender and number of the noun it describes, it has several forms.

masculine singular	meilleur
masculine plural	meilleurs
feminine singular	meilleure
feminine plural	meilleures

- Some common adjectives indicate comparison themselves and don't need the words *plus, moins,* and *aussi.* Instead of *que, à* or *de* introduces the second element of comparison.

différent de	different from
identique *à*	identical to
inférieur *à*	inferior to
pareil *à*	same as
semblable *à*	similar to
supérieur *à*	superior to

Mes intérêts sont très différents des vôtres.	My interests are very different from yours.
Ce faux sac est inférieur *à* l'orginal.	This fake bag is obviously inferior to the original.

- When comparing quatities of an item, add *de* (of) to *plus* and *moins* and use *autant de* instead of *aussi. De* is also followed by a noun, not an adjective.

Il a **plus d'expérience que** l'autre candidat.	He has more experience than the other applicant.

80

Cet endroit a **moins de parcs que** d'autres villes.	This place has less parks than other cities.
Il y a **autant de livres** ici **que** dans une bibliothèque locale.	There are as much books here as in a local library.

Superlatives

When comparing three or more elements, you use superlatives. In English, this is done by adding the article *the* to the superlative form (ending in *-est*) of the adjective. In French, you add *le, la* or *les* to *plus* or *moins* (the most/the least).

There are two ways of expressing the superlative. First is by using *le plus* or *le moins* + singular adjective. When the adjective is followed by the noun it modifies, put *le* + noun before the superlative. In both cases, the article must match the noun or adjective it is attached to.

Elle est la plus intelligente de sa classe.	She is the most intelligent in her class.
Elle est l'étudiante la plus intelligente de sa classe.	She is the most intelligent student in her class.
La plus difficile lui a été assigné.	The most difficult was assigned to her.
La tâche la plus difficile lui a été assigné.	The most difficult task was given to her.

Note: For the superlative of quatities, simply use *le plus de* + noun or *le moins de* + noun.

Il a **le plus d'expérience** parmi les quatre candidats.	He has the most experience among the four applicants.
Leur groupe a **le moins de chance**.	Their group has the least luck.

Chapter 7: Adverbs

Adverbs describe verbs, adjectives, and sometimes, other adverbs. French adverbs don't have to agree with the number and gender of the words they modify. They exist either as a single word or as an expression.

Adverbs of Time

These adverbs answer the question *quand* (when).

Adverb	Pronunciation	English
après	*ah-preh*	after
aujourd'hui	*oh-zhoor-dwee*	today
avant	*ah-vahN*	before
bientôt	*byaN-to*	soon
d'abord	*dah-bohr*	first(ly)
déjà	*day-zhah*	already
demain	*duh-maN*	tomorrow
d'habitude	*dah-bee-tewd*	usually
enfin	*ahN-faN*	finally, at last
ensuite	*ahN-sweet*	then, next
hier	*yehr*	yesterday
jamais	*zhah-meh*	never
longtemps	*lohN-tahN*	a long time
maintenant	*maNt-nahN*	now
parfois	*pahr-fwah*	sometimes, occasionally
quelquefois	*kehl-kuh-fwah*	sometimes
plus tard	*plew tahr*	later
souvent	*soo-vahN*	often
tard	*tahr*	late
tôt	*to*	early
toujours	*too-zhoor*	always, still
tout de suite	*toot sweet*	immediately, right away

Elle boit toujours du café.	She always drinks coffee.
Ils viennent souvent ici.	They come here often.

Adverbs of Place

These adverbs answer the question *où* (where).

Adverb	Pronunciation	English
à l'interieur	*ah*	inside
dehors	*duh-ohr*	outside
à côté	*ah-ko-tay*	next door, next to
à droite	*ah-drawht*	to the right
à gauche	*ah gosh*	to the left
devant	*duh-vahN*	in front
derrière	*dehr-ryehr*	behind
où	*oo*	where
ici	*ee-see*	here
loin (de)	*lawn (duh)*	far
près (de)	*preh (duh)*	close, nearby
partout	*pahr-too*	everywhere
quelque part	*kehl-kuh-pahr*	somewhere
nulle part	*newl-pahr*	nowhere
en haut	*ahN-o*	up, upstairs
en bas	*ahN-ba*	down, downstairs
au fond	*o-fohN*	at the bottom
sous	*soo*	under

Note: Many of the adverbs in the list above (and a lot more) also function as preposition. To clarify, prepositions need an object. Without it, they are adverbs. When a preposition has an object, the entire phrase acts as an adverb. For example:

Il se cache derrière.	It hides behind.
Il se cache derrière l'arbre.	It hides behind the tree.

In the first sentence, *derrière* (behind) functions as an adverb. In the second, it acts as a preposition. *Derrière l'arbre* (behind the tree) is a prepositional phrase that functions as an adverb.

Adverbs of Quantity

These adverbs answer the question *combine* (how many/how much).

Adverb	Pronunciation	English
assez (de)	*ah-say (duh)*	enough
autant	*o-tahN*	as much
beaucoup	*bo-koo*	a lot
combien	*kohN-byaN*	how many/how much
moins	*mwaN*	less
peu (de)	*puh (duh)*	little
plus	*plew*	more
presque	*prehsk*	almost
tellement	*tehl-mahN*	so much
très	*treh*	very
trop	*tro*	too much

Nous avons assez attendu.	We waited enough.
Elle est très jolie.	She is very pretty.

Adverbs of Manner

These adverbs answer the question *comment* (how) and express in what manner something is done. In English, they end in *-ly* so they're easy to recognize. In French, they end in *-ment*.

An adverb of manner is formed by adding *-ment* to the feminine singular form of an adjective or the masculine singular form of an adjective that ends in a vowel.

Adjective	Adverb	Pronunciation	English
active	activement	*ahk-teev-mahN*	actively
attentive	attentivement	*ah-tahN-teev-mahN*	attentively
complete	completement	*kohN-pleht-mahN*	completely
continuelle	continuellement	*kohN-tee-new-ehl-mahN*	continuously
douce	doucement	*doos-mahN*	gently
fière	fière	*fyehr-mahN*	proudly
heureuse	heureusement	*uh-ruhz-mahN*	fortunately
lente	lentement	*lahNt-mahN*	slowly
passionné	passionnément	*pah-syoh-nay-mahN*	enthusiastically
rapide	rapidement	*rah-peed-mahN*	quickly
sérieuse	sérieusement	*say-ree-uhz-mahN*	seriously
seule	seulement	*suhl-mahN*	only
vrai	vraiment	*vreh-mahN*	truly, really

Parle-moi lentement.	Speak to me slowly.
Nous avons écouté attentivement.	We listened attentively.

Note:

- Some adverbs are formed by replacing the final *e with é* before adding *-ment*.

Adjective	Adverb	Pronunciation	English
énorme	énormément	*ay-nohr-may-mahN*	enormously
profonde	profondément	*proh-fohN-day-mahN*	profoundly

- For adjectives ending in -*ant* and -*ent,* drop the ending and add -*amment* and -*emment,* respectively.

Adjective	Adverb	Pronunciation	English
constant	constamment	*kohN-stah-mahN*	constantly
courant	couramment	*koo-rah-mahN*	fluently
évident	évidemment	*ay-vee-deh-mahN*	evidently
prudent	prudemment	*prew-deh-mahN*	prudenly
recent	récemment	*ray-seh-mahN*	recently

- Some adverbs have distinct forms from adjectives

Adjective	English	Adverb	English
bon	good	bien	well
bref	brief	brièvement	briefly
gentil	kind	gentiment	kindly
mauvais	bad	mal	badly
meilleur	better	mieux	better
rapide	fast	vite *	quickly

* *rapidement* also exists

- Some adjectives are used as adverbs in certain expressions. The adverbs mean a bit differently from the adjective and they don't agree with anything.

Adjective	English	Adverb	English
bas	low	parler bas	to speak softly

bon	good	sentir bon	to smell good
cher	expensive	coùter cher	to cost a lot
clair	clear	voir clair	to see clearly
dur	hard	travailler dur	to work hard
fort	strong	parler fort	to speak loud
mauvais	bad	sentir mauvais	to smell bad

- If you're having a hard time in coming up with the right adverb of manner, or when one just doesn't exist, use the phrases *d'une manière* (in a manner) or *d'une façon* (in a fashion) + feminine singular adjective.

Elle joue d'une manière intelligente.	She plays intelligently.
Il parle d'une façon hautaine.	He speaks in a haughty fashion.

Proper Placing of Adverbs

Adverbs are commonly placed after the word they modify. But they move around in the sentence depending on whether they modify a verb, an adjective, or another adverb.

- An adverb modifying a verb in simple tense is placed after the verb.

Je mange rarement de la viande.	I rarely eat meat.
Nous travaillons dur.	We work hard.

- An adverb modifying a verb in a *passé composé* tense, is placed after the second verb.

Il a conduit prudemment.	He drove carefully.

| Ils ont marché tranquillement. | They walked quietly. |

However, some very common adverbs don't follow this pattern. Instead, they go between the helping verb and the past participle. These adverbs are *bien* (well), *beaucoup* (much), *déjà* (already), *mal* (badly), *probablement* (probably), *tellement* (so much), *toujours* (always), *vite* (quickly), and *vraiment* (really).

- An adverb modifying a verb in the form *aller* + infinitive is placed after the conjugated form of *aller*.

| Ils vont certainement gagner. | They're definitely going to win. |
| Nous allons évidemment perdre. | We're obviously going to lose. |

- An adverb modifying another adverb or an adjective is placed before those that it modifies.

| Vous êtes vraiment belle. | You're really beautiful. |
| Il écrit très bien. | He writes very well. |

- Long adverbs such as *attentivement* (attentively) and *continuellement* (continuously) are usually placed at the end of a sentence, at times separated from the conjugated verb.

- Unlike in English, French adverbs can never be placed after the subject.

Chapter 8: Types of Sentences

Now that you've learned about the different parts of speech, you're ready to create your own French sentences.

Une phrase (a sentence) is a group of words that expresses a complete thought. At a minimum, it has a subject and a verb, although there are cases where the subject is not stated but implied. The subject is the person(s) or thing(s) that performs the action. The predicate is the part of the sentence that states something about the subject and usually starts with the verb.

	Nous habitons en France.	We live in France.
Subject	Nou	We
Predicate	habitons en France	live in France

There are four types of French sentences: *phrase declarative* or *assertive* (statement), *phrase interrogative* (question), *phrase exclamative* (exclamation), and *phrase imperative* (command). But before learning about these different types of sentences, you need to be familiar with the more pronouns.

Object Pronouns

In Chapter 5, you learned about subject pronouns – pronouns that are used as subject of the verb. In many cases, you need to use an object pronoun.

Verbs may or may not need an object but many will not make sense without an object attached to it in a sentence. The object – which is either a noun or a pronoun - receives the action of the verb directly or indirectly.

Direct objects answer the question *what* or *whom* the subject is acting upon. They may refer to people, objects, places, or ideas. In contrast, indirect objects answer the question *for whom* or *to whom* the subject is doing something. In French, indirect objects may only refer to people or other animate nouns.

Direct Object Pronouns			Indirect Object Pronouns		
me	me (m')	*muh*	(to) me	me (m')	*muh*
you	te (t')	*tuh*	(to) you	te (t')	*tuh*
he, it	le (l')	*luh*	(to) him	lui	*lwee*
her, it	la (l')	*lah*	(to her)	lui	*lwee*
us	nous	*noo*	(to) us	nous	*noo*
you	vous	*voo*	(to) you	vous	*voo*
them	les	*lay*	(to) them	leur	*luhr*

Note that direct and indirect object pronouns are the same except for the third person singular and plural. Also note that the singular form of indirect object pronouns has no gender distinction.

Direct pronouns are used when you can go straight from a verb to its object without needing a preposition like *to* or *for*. If the object is anything that's not animated, you also need to use a direct pronoun.

Je **l'**ai jeté.	I threw it.
Je **le** aime.	I like him.

Too often in English, *to* or *for* is assumed and not used. In these cases, you must use an indirect object.

Je **lui** ai donné des fleurs.	I gave (to) her flowers.
Je **leur** ai acheté de nouvelles chaussures.	I bought (for) them new shoes.

Some verbs are always followed by the preposition *à* (*au, la, l',* or *aux*) + [name of or reference to a person], indicating that the object is indirect. Thus, you need to use an indirect object pronoun when replacing the noun.

announcer	to announce to
donner	to give to
dire à	to tell to
obéir à quelqu'un	to obey someone
parler à	to talk to
poser des questions à quelqu'un	to ask someone questions
prêter à	to lend to
rendre visite à	to pay a visit to
ressembler à quelqu'un	to ressemble someone
téléphoner à quelqu'un	to call someone

Je vais **lui** poser une question.	I will ask her a question.
Il **leur** parlera.	He will talk to them.

When the verb is followed by a preposition other than à, different pronouns are used.

moi	me	*nous*	us
toi	you	*vous*	you
elle	her	*elles*	them *f.*
lui	him	*eux*	them *m.*

Il marche **vers** eux.	He is walking toward them.
Elle sort **avec** moi.	She is going out with me.

Position of Pronouns

As you can see from the preceding examples, French object pronouns are placed before the verb they are tied to. For sentences with compound verbs, they are put before the verb they actually go with.

In the *passé compose*, the whole auxiliary + past participle is considered the verb so the pronoun is placed before them. In the *futur proche* (conjugated *aller* + *infinitive*), the verb that has an object is the infinitive so the pronoun is placed between the two verbs.

Je **lui** air rendu visite en France.	I visited her in France.
Ils vont **me** rendre visite le mois prochain.	They are going to visit me next month.

Phrase Declarative

The most common type of sentence is the statement or declarative sentence. Statement are expressed either in affirmative or negative manner. Almost all of the examples in the previous chapters are affirmative sentences.

Negative Sentences

To form a negative sentence, French always uses two negative words – *ne,* a word that doesn't have an English translation, and *pas* (not). *Ne* + conjugated verb + *pas* makes a sentence negative.

Nous **ne** jouons **pas** au basket.	We don't like football.
Cette phrase **n'**est **pas** positive.	This sentence is not positive.

Note that in the second example, the conjugated verb (*est*) starts with a vowel so *ne* becomes *n'*. *Pas* can be replaced by these negative words:

aucun/aucune + noun	no, none, not any
jamais	never
même pas	not even
ni ... ni	neither ... nor
nulle part	nowhere
pas encore	not yet
pas grand-chose	not much
pas non plus	either, neither
personne	nobody, no one
plus	no longer, not any more
rien	nothing

Nous **n'avons plus** d'eau.	We don't have any more water.
Elle **ne** sait **même pas**.	She doesn't even know.
Ils **n'aiment personne**.	They don't like anybody.

Notes:

- When the verb is in the infinitive form, the two negative words stick together and are followed by the infinitive.

Je choisis de **ne pas** jouer.	I choose not to play.
Je prévois de **ne pas** te rejoindre.	I plan not to join you.

- When the subject of the sentence is *personne* (nobody/no one) or *rien* (nothing), start the sentence with the negative word just like in English and proceed with *ne* followed by the verb.

| Rien ne dure éternellement. | Nothing lasts forever. |
| Personne ne répond au telephone. | Nobody answers the phone. |

- In some cases, particularly in conversations, you don't need a complete sentence to express what you mean. Here are some negative expressions that you may find useful.

jamais plus	never again
moi non plus	me neither
pas du tout	not at all
pas grand-chose	not much
pas maintenant	not now
pas question	no way

Phrase Interrogative

In order to communicate properly, you also need to know how to ask questions. Questions come in two varieties: the simple yes-or-no questions and the information questions.

Yes-or-No Questions

In English, you normally begin with *Do you* when asking a yes-or-no question in present tense. In French, there are a number of ways to do so.

Intonation

The easiest way to express a question is by simply chaging your intonation. Note that in written form, you just add a question mark to a *phrase declarative*. And because both sentences are worded in the same manner, the only way for the other person to know that you're asking a question is if you raise your voice at the end of the sentence.

Tu es heureux.	You're happy.
Tu es heureux?	Are you happy?
Tu travailles le vendredi	You're working on Friday.
Tu travailles le vendredi?	Are you working on Friday?

Est-ce que

Another way of forming a question in French is by putting the tag *est-ce que* at the start of the sentence and ending it with a question mark. *Est-ce que* doesn't get translated in English but in French, it indicates that a question follows. Notice that the phrase that comes after *est-ce que* is the same as the declarative form.

Elle est allée à la plage.	She went to the beach.
Est-ce qu'elle est allée à la plage.	Did she go to the beach?
Le chien dort sur le canapé.	The dog is sleeping on the couch.
Est-ce que le chien dort sur le canapé?	Is the dog sleeping on the couch?

Note that when *est-ce-que* is followed by a subject beginning with a vowel, it changes to *est-ce-qu'*.

N'est-ce pas?

N'est-ce pas (*nehs pah*) translates to isn't that so. You can form a question by adding at the end of the sentence.

Ils l'ont fait, n'est-ce pas?	They did it, didn't they (isn't that so)?
Elle t'aime, n'est-ce pas?	She loves you, doesn't she? (isn't that so)?

Inversion

Inversion is a bit complex and is used far more often in writing than in conversation. It is done by reversing the order of the subject pronoun and the conjugated verb. The rules of inversion are somewhat complicated but the methods that follow simplify them for you.

- Never invert with *je* and the verb. It's quite formal and awkward so it's extremely rarely used.

- Invert conjugated verbs only with subject pronouns. Never invert with nouns.

Vous-parlez français.	You speak French.
Parlez-vous français?	Do you speak French?

- When inverting *il* or *elle* with a conjugated verb that ends with a vowel, you will need to add a -*t*- in between the inverted verb and subject pronoun. This is done for pronunciation's sake.

Travaille-**t**-il dans un bureau?	Does he work in an office?
Aime-**t**-elle les chats?	Does she like cats?

Note: To answer a yes-or-no question, use *oui* (yes) and *non* (no) if the question is positive. If the question is negative, use *si* for yes.

Information Questions

When you need more than a simple yes or no for an answer, you ask an information question. Like in English, it starts with an interrogative word, which is technically an adverb or adjective.

French	Pronunciation	English
qui, qee	*kee*	who, whom
que, qu'est-ce que	*kuh, kehs-kuh*	what
quand	*kahN*	when
où	*oo*	where
comment	*kohN-mahN*	how
pourquoi	*poor-kwah*	why
à quelle heure	*ah-kehl-uhr*	at what time
à qui	*ah-kee*	to whom
à quoi	*ah-kwah*	to what
avec qui	*ah-vehk-kee*	with whom
avec quoi	*ah-vehk-kwah*	with what
de qui	*duh-kee*	of, about, from whom
combien (de + noun)	*kohN-byaN (duh)*	how much, how many
d' où	*doo*	from where
quell + noun	*kehl*	what, which

Forming an informative question is much like forming a yes-or-no-question. You just need to add the question word or expression at the beginning.

Aimes-tu les chats?	Do you like cats?
Pourquoi aimes-tu les chats?	Why do you like cats?
Es-tu allé en France?	Did you go to France?
Quand es-tu allé en France?	When did you go to France?

What?

In French, there are several ways in which you can ask a question with what: *que, qu'est-ce qui, qu'est ce que,* and *quel.*

- Use *qu'est-ce qui* when the answer to the question is the subject of the verb. If you can't find a noun or pronoun functioning as the subject (just like in the second example below), then the answer itself is the subject.

Qu'est-ce qui se cache dans la boîte? Un chat se cache dans la boîte.	Q: What hides in the box? A: **A cat** hides in the box.
Qu'est-ce qui est arrivé? La voiture est en panne.	Q: What happened? A: **The car broke down.**

- Use *qu'est-ce que* when the answer to the question is the object of the verb.

Qu'est-ce que tu veux? Je veux aller à Paris.	Q: What do you want? A: I want **to go** to Paris.
Qu'est-ce que vous obtenez? J'ai un nouveau livre.	Q: What did you get? A: I got a new **book**.

- *Que* is the short version of *qu'est-ce que*. You'll probably never use it in conversation because it requires inversion.

Qu'as-tu mange?	What did you eat?
Que vas-tu faire?	What will you do?

- *Quel,* meaning which or what, is an interrogative adjective and is used when the answer is in the context of an option. *Quel* is an adjective so it has different forms to agree with the gender and number of the *what*. These are: *quel* (masculine singular), *quels* (masculine plural), *quelle* (feminine singular), and *quelles* (feminine plural).

Quels films voulez-vous voir?	Which movies do you want to see?
Quelle est ta robe préférée?	Which is your favorite dress?

Phrase Exclamative

Sentences expressing enthusiasm and surprise are called *phrase exclamative*. They usually look just like statements and the only difference is they have an exclamation point instead of a period.

Je suis en colère!	I'm angry!
J'ai peur!	I'm scared!

Similar to English, *phrase exclamative* is also often expressed with question words such as *quoi* (what), *que* (how + adjective), and *quel* (what + noun). *Comme* literally means *as* but when used for exclamations, it translates to *how*.

Quel beau garcon.	What a handsome boy!
Comme il est genial.	How great he is!
Quelle aventure!	What an adventure!

- When *quel* is used, it must agree with the gender and number of the noun that comes after it. Also note that no article precedes the noun. An adjective can be placed before the noun to make things specific.

Quelle belle journée!	What a beautiful day!
Quels arbres énormes!	What huge trees!

- Sometimes, you can just include an adjective when expressing something that is quite obvious. In English, you can say something like, *How crazy!*, skipping not just the noun but also the verb. In contrast, you can't leave out the verb in French, which is *c'est* (it is). You can use either *comme* or *que* but you can also skip them.

Comme c'est joli!	How pretty!
Que c'est joli!	How pretty!
C'est joli!	That's pretty!

There are many French *phrase exclamative* considered a mild slang that you can use to express strong emotions.

French	Pronunciation	English
Allez!	*ah-lay*	Oh, c'mon!
Assez de bêtises!	*ah-say-duh-beh-teez*	Knock it off!
Bien sur!	*byaN-sewr*	Of course!
Bon débarras!	*bohN-day-bah-rah*	Good riddance!
Cela dépasse le bornes!	*suh-lah-day-pahs-lay-bohrn*	That's going too far!
C'est le cas de le dire!	*seh-luh-kah-duh-luh-deer*	You can say that again!
C'est nul!	*seh-newl*	That sucks!
C'est trop fort!	*seh-tro-fohr*	You're too much!
Ça, c'est le comble!	*sah-seh-luh-kuhNbl*	That's the last straw!
Ça me fait rager!	*sah-me-feh-rah-zhay*	That infuriates me!
Ça m'inquiète!	*sah-maN-kee-yeht*	That bugs me!
Ça suffit!	*sah-sew-fee*	Cut it out!
Décide-toi!	*day-seed-twah*	Make up your mind!
(Ferme) ta gueule!	*fehr-muh-tah-guhl*	Shut up!
Grâce au ciel!	*grahs-o-syehl*	Thank heavens!
Honte à toi!	*ohN-tah-twah*	Shame on you!
J'en ai marre!	*zhahN-nay-mahr*	I've had it up to here!
Je n'en reviens pas!	*zhuh-nahN-ruh-vyaN-pah*	I can't get over it!
Laisse-moi tranquille!	*lehs-mwah-trahN-keel*	Leave me alone!
Mêle-toi de tes affaires!	*mehl-twah-duh-tay-zah-fehr*	Mind your own business!
N'importe!	*naN-pohrt*	Never mind!

Pas question!	*pah-kehs-tyohN*	No way!
Ras le bol!	*rah-luh-bohl*	I'm really fed up!
Reste couvert!	*rehst-koo-vehr*	Keep your shirt on!
Tu me rends fou (folle)!	*tew-muh-rahN-foo (fohl)*	You're driving me nuts!
Tu parles!	*tew-pahrl*	Big deal! You must be kidding!
Un peu!	*uhN-puh*	You bet!
Va-t'en!	*vah-tuhN*	Go away!

Phrase imperative

A *phrase imperative* expresses something that must be done. In this type of sentence, the *impératif* form of verb is used.

Impératif

The *impératif* exists in three forms: first person plural corresponding to nous, second person singular corresponding to *tu,* and second person plural corresponding to *vous.* Because you don't use the subject pronouns when expressing a command, it's important to use the right form of verb. It's the only way for the receiver(s) to know that the command is directed at them. The good news is that it's quite easy to conjugate to the *impératif* form.

- For -*er* verbs, drop the -*s* in the present tense form corresponding to *tu.* Use the same form for *nous* and *vous.*

Present Tense	*Impératif*	Present Tense	*Impératif*
tu trouves	trouve	tu vas	va
nous trouvons	trouvons	nous allons	allons
vous trouvez	trouvez	vous allez	allez

- For regular *-ir* and *-re* verbs, use the present tense form corresponding to *tu, nous,* and *vous.*

Present Tense	*Impératif*	Present Tense	*Impératif*
tu viens	viens	tu dis	dis
nous venons	venons	tu disons	disowns
vous venez	venez	tu disent	dites

- There are three common verbs that use a different form for the *impératif*. These are *avoir* (to have), *être* (to be), and *savoir* (to know).

	Avoir	Être	Savoir
tu	aie	sois	sache
nous	ayons	soyons	sachons
vous	ayez	soyez	sachez

Attendre Jack.	Wait for Jack.
Attendons Jack.	Let's wait for Jack.
Attendez Jack.	(You all) wait for Jack.

- To give a negative command, simply surround the *impératif* with *ne* and *pas* (or another negative expression).

Ne traversez pas la rue.	Don't cross the street.
Ne va nulle part.	Don't go anywhere.

Position of Pronouns

In many cases, the *impératif* is followed by an object pronoun, like Give *me* that./Don't give *me* that. In French, the position of the object pronoun depends on whether the command is affirmative or negative.

- In affirmative commands, object pronouns are located after the *impératif* and attached to it with a hyphen. *Me* and *te* are transformed to *moi* and *toi*.

Excusez-moi.	Excuse me.
Donne-leur à manger.	Give them food.

- In negative commands, the object pronun is placed before the *impératif* and after the word *ne*. *Me* and *te* remains the same.

Ne m'oublie pas.	Don't forget me.
Ne la laisse pas partir.	Don't let her go.

Chapter 9: Idioms and Idiomatic Expressions

Idioms are words or expressions whose meanings don't reflect the individual meaning of the words they're made of. Because they can't be easily understood, those who are just starting to learn the language avoid them. However, a lot of them are actually used in everyday situations. So if you want to express yourself and speak in a foreign language like a native speaker, it's important to learn idioms.

A lot of idioms are formed with the words *avoir*, *être*, *avoir*, and a few more verbs. When using these verbs, make sure that you conjugate them properly to agree with the number and tense.

French	Pronunciation	English
apprendre par cœur	*ah-prahNdr-pahr-kuhr*	to memorize
avoir besoin de	*ah-vwahr-buh-zwaN-duh*	to need
avoir chaud	*ah-vwahr-sho*	to be warm
avoir envie de	*ah-vwahr-ahN-vee-duh*	to feel like
avoir faim	*ah-vwahr-faN*	to be hungry
avoir froid	*ah-vwahr-frwah*	to be cold
avoir mal (à + body part)	*ah-vwahr-mahl (ah)*	to have a pain
avoir peur (de)	*ah-vwahr-puhr (duh)*	to be afraid of
avoir raison	*ah-vwahr-reh-zohN*	to be right
avoir soif	*ah-vwahr-swahf*	to be thirsty
avoir tort	*ah-vwahr-tohr*	to be wrong
avoir de la chance	*ah-vwahr-duh-lah-shahNs*	to be lucky
avoir l'occasion de	*ah-vwhar-loh-kah-*	to have the

	zyohN-du	opportunity to
avoir le temps de	*ah-vwahr-luh-tahN-duh*	to have the time to
être à	*ehtr-ah*	to belong to
être d'accord (avec)	*ehtr-dah-kohr (ah-vehk)*	to agree (with)
être en train de	*ehtr-ahN-traN-duh*	to be busy (doing something)
être sur le point de	*ehtr-sewr-luh-pwaN-duh*	to be about to
y être	*ee-ehtr*	to understand, to see
faire beau	*fehr-bo*	to be nice weather
faire chaud	*fehr-cho*	to be hot weather
faire du vent	*fehr-dew-vahN*	to be windy
faire frais	*fehr-freh*	to be cool weather
faire froid	*fehr-frwah*	to be cold weather
fair mauvais	*feh-mo-veh*	to be bad weather
faire attention (à)	*fehr-ah-than-syohN (ah)*	to pay attention (to)
faire des achats	*fehr-day-zah-shah*	to go shopping
faire la connaissance de	*fehr-lah-koh-neh-sahNs-duh*	to be acquainted with
faire une promenade	*fehr-ewn-prohm-nahd*	to take a walk, a ride
faire un voyage	*fehr-uhN-vwah-yahzh*	to take a trip
n'en pouvoir plus	*nahN-poo-vwahr-plew*	to be exhausted
valoir la peine (de + infinitive)	*vah-lwahr-lah-pehn (duh)*	to be worthwhile
valoir mieux	*vah-lwahr-myuh*	to be better

venir de	*vuh-neer-duh*	to have just
vouloir dire	*voo-lwahr-deer*	to mean

Here are a few examples of these idioms in action.

Cet achat en **valait la peine**.	That purchase was worth it.
J'etais sur le point de partir quand tu es arrivé.	I was about to leave when you arrived.
Je **veux dire**, je ne l'ai pas fait.	I mean, I didn't do it.
Vous devez **fair attention à** ce que vous faites.	You need to pay attention to whatever you're doing.
Il **fait** toujours **froid** ici.	It's always cold here.
J'avais raison mais tu ne me croyais pas.	I was right but you didn't believe me.

Some idiomatic expressions start with a preposition. They may refer to time, location, direction, and travel. Others can be used to express your opinions or feelings about things.

French	Pronunciation	English
à + time expression	*ah*	good-bye, until
à demain	*ah-duh-maN*	see you tomorrow
à jamais	*ah-zhah-meh*	forever
à l'heure	*ah-luhr*	on time
à peu près	*ah-puh-preh*	about, approximately, nearly
à propos de, au sujet de	*ah-proh-po-duh, o-soo-heh-duh*	about, concerning
à quoi bon + infinitive	*ah-kwah-bohN*	what's the use of ...?
à tout à l'heure	*ah-too-lah-luhr*	see you in a little while
bon marché	*bohN-mahr-shay*	cheap
C'est entendu.	*seh-tahN-tahN-dew*	It's agreed.

106

c'est-à-dire	seh-tah-deer	that's to say
Cela m'est égal.	seh-lah-meh-tay-gahl	It makes no difference to me.
Cela ne fait rien.	suh-lah-nuh-feh-ryaN	That doesn't matter.
de bonne heure	duh-boh-nuhr	early
de la part de	duh-lah-pahr-duh	on behalf of, from
de nouveau	duh-noo-vo	again
Il n'y a pas de quoi.	eel-nyah-pah-duh-kwah	Don't mention it.
en effet	ahN-neh-feh	(yes) indeed, as a matter of fact
en même temps	ahN-mehm-than	at the same time
en retard	ahN-ruh-tahr	late, not on time
en tout cas	ahN-too-kah	in any case, at any rate
encore une fois	ahN-kohr-ewn-fwah	again
et ainsi de suite	ay-aN-see-duh-sweet	and so forth
grâce à	grahs-ah	thanks to
meilleur marché	meh-yuhr-mahr-shay	cheaper
n'importe	naN-pohrt	no matter
par conséquent	pahr-kohN-say-kahN	consequently, therefore
par exemple	pahr-ehg-zahNpl	for example
par hasard	pahr-ah-zahr	by chance
peu à peu	puh-ah-puh	gradually, little by little
peut-être	puh-tehtr	maybe, perhaps
quant â	kahN-tah	as for
sans doute	sahN-doot	without a doubt
tant mieux	than-myuh	so much the better
tant pis	than-pee	so much the worse, too bad
tous (les) deux	too (lay) duh	both
tout à (d'un) coup	too-tah (duhN) koo	suddenly
tout à fait	too-tah-feh	entirely, quite
tout de même	tood-mehm	all the same

| tout de suite | *toot-sweet* | immediately |
| tout le monde | *too-luh-mohNd* | everybody |

And here are a few examples showing how these idioms are used.

Il a quelque chose pour **tout le monde.**	He's got something for everybody.
Nous sommes arrivés **de bonne heure.**	We arrived early.
Tant pis il ne soit pas là pour voir ça.	Too bad he's not here to see this.
Sans doute, nous allons gagner.	Without doubt, we're going to win.
Tu es **en retard.**	You're late.
Nous devons parler **à propos** l'avenir.	We must talk about the future.

And here are some more French idiomatic expressions. If you're someone who expresses yourself using a lot of idioms, you'll find the following list interesting.

French Idiom	Equivalent English Expression / Description
C'est dommage.	That's a shame.
Je dis ça, je dis rien.	Just saying.
Ne pas mettre tous ses œufs dans le même panier.	Don't put your eggs in one basket.
C'est du gateau.	Piece of cake.
Mieux vaut tard que jamais.	Better late than never.
Plus facile à dire qu'á faire.	Easier said than done.
(Ce n'est pas) ma tasse de thé.	(It's not) my cup of tea.
(Me) Passer sur le corps.	Over my dead body.
avoir le cafard	to feel down or sad
couper les cheveux en quatre	to be full of yourself
péter un plomb	to get really angry

prendre quelqu'un la main dans le sac	to catch someone red-handed
avoir la gueule de bois	to have a hangover
coûter les yeux de la tête	to cost an arm and a leg
ne rien savoir faire de ses dix doigts	(someone who is) completely useless
arriver comme un cheveu sur la soupe	to arrive at the most awkward moment
mettre son grain de sel	to give (someone) an unsolicited opinion
faire la grasse matinée	to sleep in
un coup de foudre	love at first sight / head over heels
poser un lapin à quelqu'un	to stand someone up
avoir les yeux plus gros que le ventre	to have eyes bigger than the stomach

Chapter 10: Everyday French

By now, you should already be familiar with the pronunciation of French words. If not, you can always go back to Chapter 1 and recall how to properly pronounce words. In case you're still unsure, don't worry because a lot of the examples in this chapter still include pronunciation guide.

Greetings, General Conversations, and Farewells

Bonjour!	Hello! / Good morning!
Bonsoir!	Good evening! / Hello!
Salut!	Hi! (when seeing someone again later in the day) / Bye!
Coucou!	Hey! (very informal)
Âllo!	Hello! (for answering the phone)
Ça fait longtemps, dis donc.	Long time no see. / It's been a while.
(Comment) ça va?	How are you?
Comment allez-vous?	How are you?
Quoi de neuf?	What's up?
I'm fine, thank you.	Je vais bien, merci.
Tres bien.	Very well.
Pas mal.	Not bad.
Comme ci, comme ça.	So-so.
What about you?	Et vous?
Bonne chance.	Good luck.
Oui.	Yes
Non.	No.
S'il vous plaît.	Please.
Je suis désolé.	I'm sorry.
Félicitations!	Congratulations!

Bon anniversaire!	Happy birthday!
See you later.	À bientôt. / À plus.
See you tomorrow.	À demain.
Au revoir.	Goodbye.
Ciao!	See ya!
Prenez soins de vous. / Prends soins de toi. (informal)	Take care.
Enchanté(e).	Nice to meet you.
Au Plaisir de vous revoir.	Hope to see you again.
Merci.	Thank you.
Je vous en prie. / De rien.	You're welcome.
Madame / Mme	Madam / Mrs.
Mademoiselle / Mlle	Miss
Monsieur / M.	Mister / Mr. / Sir

Remember that how you talk in French depends on who you're talking to and the social setting. Always use the polite form with people you're meeting for the first time or people you're supposed to give respect to and when you're in a business setting. When meeting friends, the French usually greet each other with *les bises* (kisses). Handshakes are reserved for business or formal settings.

About Yourself

Comment vous appelez-vous? / Comment t'appelles-tu? (informal)	What's your name?
Je m'appelle ...	My name is ...

The literal English translation of *Comment vous appelez-vous?* / *Comment t'appelles-tu?* is How do you call yourself? When you reply with *Je m'appelle Jack*, you're actually saying I call myself Jack.

Quel âge avez-vous? / Quel âge as-tu? (informal)	How old are you?
J'ai (vant) ans.	I'm (20) years old.

Quel âge avez-vous? / *Quel âge as-tu?* also don't translate literally to How old are you? The French actually ask what age you have. *J'ai (vant) ans* means I have (twenty) years.

Vous êtes d'où?	Where are you from?
Je suis des États-Unis.	I'm from the United States.

Family Members

English	French	Pronunciation
mother	la mère	*lah-mehr*
father	le père	*luh-pehr*
grandmother	la grand-mère	*lah-graN-mehr*
grandfather	le grand-père	*luh-grahN-pehr*
mother-in-law	la belle-mère	*lah-behl-mehr*
father-in-law	le beau- père	*luh-bo-pehr*
child	l'enfant	*lahN-fahN*
sister	la sœur	*lah-suhr*

brother	le frère	*luh-frehr*
stepsister	la demi-sœur	*lah-duh-mee-suhr*
stepbrother	le demi-frère	*luh-duh-mee-frehr*
stepdaughter, daughter-in-law	la belle-fille	*lah-behl-fee-y*
stepson, son-in-law	le beau-fils	*luh-bo-fees*
son-in-law	le gendre	*luh-zhahNdr*
daughter	la fille	*lah-fee-y*
son	la fils	*luh-fees*
aunt	la tante	*lah-tahNt*
uncle	l'oncle	*lohNkl*
cousin	la cousine / le cousin	*lah-koo-zeen / luh-koo-zaN*
niece	la niece	*lah-nyehs*
nephew	le neveu	*luh-nuh-vuh*
wife	la femme	*lah-fahm*
husband	le mari	*luh-mah-ree*
girlfriend	la petite amie	*lah-puh-tee tah-mee*
boyfriend	le petit ami	*luh-puh-tee-tah-mee*

When talking about a family member, you say "my father" or "my cousin" using possessive adjectives which are discussed in Chapter 6. But what if you want to talk about your sister's boyfriend or your child's favorite toy? The French don't use apostrophes to express possession. Instead, they use the preposition *de* which means *of.*

le petit ami de ma sœur	my sister's boyfriend
jouet préféré de mon enfant	my childs favorite toy

113

Professions

English	French	Pronunciation
What is your profession?	Que lest votre métier?	*kehl-eh-vohtr-may-tyay*
I'm an ...	Je suis ...	*zhuh-swee*
accountant	comptable	*kohN-tahbl*
dentist	dentist *m.*	*dehN-teest*
doctor	docteur *m.*	*dohk-tuhr*
hairdresser	coiffeur / coiffeuse	*kwah-fuhr / kwah-fuhz*
lawyer	avocat(e)	*ah-voh-kah(t)*
manager	gérant(e)	*zhay-rahN(t)*
nurse	infirmier / infirmière	*aN-feer-myay / ahN-feer-myehr*
physician	médecin	*mayd-saN*
police officer	agent de police *m.*	*ah-zhahN-duh-poh-lees*
secretary	secrétaire	*seh-kray-tehr*

When You Don't Understand

When talking to French speakers, you may find it hard to understand what they're saying. Maybe it's their accent, they talk too fast, or you're encountering unfamiliar words especially now that you're only starting to learn the language. Here are some phrases and sentences that can help you if you need more information or clarification.

French	Pronunciation	English
Pardon ...	*pahr-dohN*	Pardon me ...
Je ne comprends pas.	*zhuh-nuh-kohN-prahN-pah*	I don't understand.
Je ne vous (t') ai pas entendu.	*zhuh-nuh-voo-zay (tay) pah-zahN-tahN-dew*	I didn't hear you.

114

Parlez (Parle) plus lentement, s'il vous plaît.	*pahr-lay (pahrl) plew-lahNt-mahN*	Please speak more slowly.
Qu'est-ce que vous avez (tu as) dit?	*kehs-kuh-voo-zah-vay (tew ah)-dee*	What did you say?
Répétéz (Répète), s'il vous (te) plaît.	*ray-pay-tay (ray-peht) seel-voo (tuh) pleh*	Please repeat it.

Note: *Words in parenthesis are used for familiar speech.*

What's the Weather Today?

French	Pronunciation	English
Quel temps fait-il aujourd'hui?	*kehl-than-feh-tee-luh-zhoor-dwee*	What's the weather today?
Il fait beau.	*eel-feh-bo*	It's nice.
Il fait chaud.	*eel-feh-sho*	It's hot.
Il fait du soleil.	*eel-feh-dew-soh-lehy*	It's sunny.
If fait mauvais.	*eel-feh-moh-veh*	It's bad weather.
Il fait frais.	*eel-feh-freh*	It's cool.
Il fait froid.	*eel-feh-frwah*	It's cold.
Il fait du vent.	*eel-feh-dew-vahN*	It's windy.
If fait humide.	*eel-feh-tew-meed*	It's humid.
Il y a du brouillard.	*eel-yah-dew-broo-yahr*	It's foggy.
Il y a des nuages.	*eel-yah-des-nuages*	It's cloudy.
Il pleut.	*eel-pleut*	It's raining.
Il pleut à verse.	*eel-pluh-ah-vehrs*	It's pouring.
Il neige.	*eel-nehzh*	It's snowing.
Il y a de la grêle.	*eel-yah-duh-lah-grehl*	There's hail.
Le ciel est couvert.	*luh-syehl-eh-koo-vehr*	It's overcast.

When talking about the weather, the French don't use the verb *être* (to be) unlike in English. They use *faire* (to make/to do) so the literal English translation of *Il fait froid* is It makes cold.

Remember that in French-speaking countries, temperature is measured and expressed in Celsius instead of Fahrenheit. So when you hear someone say *Il fait vingt,* don't assume that it's freezing out there. *Il fait vraiment beau.*

Y and *En*

You've learned how to replace nouns with direct and indirect pronouns from the previous chapters. However, there are some instances when you have to change not just one word but a whole phrase. In French, there are special pronouns used to replace prepositional phrases: *y* and *en.*

Y, which means *there,* generally replaces *à* and its many forms, *chez, contre* (against), *dans* (in), *derrière* (behind), *devant* (in front of), *en* (in), *entre* (between), *sous* (under), *sur* (on), and *vers* (toward). It can also mean it or them, on it/them, in it/them, or to it/them.

J'ai laissé le livre sur la table.	I left the book on the table.
J'ai y laissé le livre.	I left the book there.
Est-elle dans sa chambre?	Is she in her room?
Oui, elle est dans sa chambre.	Yes, she's in her room.
Oui, elle y est.	Yes, she's there.
Il s'est assis à l'ombre d'un énorme arbre.	He sat under the shade of a huge tree.
Il s'est y assis.	He sat there.

En refers to previously mentioned places or things. It usually takes the place of *de* + noun and could mean from there, about it/them, any of it/them, or from it/them.

Nous avons parlé du voyage. Nous en avons parlé.	We spoke about the trip. We spoke about it.
Il veut du gâteau au chocolat. Il en veut.	He wants some chocolate cake. He wants some of them.
Avez-vous un nouveau livre? Oui, j'en ai.	Do you have any new book? Yes, I do.

Y and *en* are usually placed before the conjugated verb. Although it may not have an equivalent or is not stated in English, *en* is always expressed in French, as showed in the last example above.

Everyday Conversations

Here are some of the most common sentences that you use in conversatoin a regular basis.

Je suis prêt.	I'm ready.
Attends-moi.	Wait for me.
Je vous attends.	I'm waiting for you.
Il est temps de partir.	It's time to go.
J'ai faim. Mangeons.	I'm hungry. Let's eat.
Avez-vous faim?	Are you hungry?
Je ne fais jamais la cuisine.	I never cook.
Passe le poivre, s'il te plaît.	Pass the pepper, please.
Je n'ai pas d'argent liquide.	I don't have cash.
Celui-ci est meilleur marché que celui-la.	This one is cheaper than that one.

Ça me va?	Does it fit me?
Qui est à l'appareil?	Who's calling?
C'est pour vous.	It's for you.
Donne-moi ton numéro.	Give me your number.
Que veux-tu? / Qu'est-ce que tu veux?	What do you want?
Qu'est-ce qui s'est passé?	What happened?
Tu te sens bien?	Do you feel well?
Lave-toi les mains.	Wash your hands.
Où est-ce que ça fait mal?	Where does it hurt?
Permettez-moi de vous aider.	Let me help you.
Amuse-toi bein!	Have fun!
Bon voyage!	Have a good trip!
Attachez votre ceinture de sécurité.	Buckle up.
Le spectacle va commencer.	The show is about to start.
Je serai là dans quelques minutes.	I'll be there in a few minutes.
Je vais être en retard.	I'll be late.
Nous sommes en retard à cause d'un bouchon.	We're late because of a traffic jam.
Il est l'heure de se réveiller.	It's time to wake up.
Vous avez l'heure?	Do you have the time?
Quel jour sommes-nous?	What day is it today?
Avez-vous vu cette?	Have you seen this?
Que veut dire ça.	What does that mean?
Je t'aime.	I love you.
Dites-moi ce que vous pensez.	Tell me what you think.
C'est tout?	Is that all?
Pas de problème.	No problem.
Depuis quand?	Since when?
Je te tiens au courant.	I'll let you know.
Ne t'inquiète pas.	Don't worry.

Pas pour moi.	Not for me.
Quels sont vos plans ce weekend?	What are your plans this weekend?
Puis-je faire ça?	Can I do that?
Que voulez-vous faire?	What do you want to do?
Nous allons boire un verre.	We're going out for a drink.
Où on se retrouve?	Where do we meet?
Où allez-vous?	Where do you live?
Comment ça va votre famille?	How's your family?
Ça va le travaille?	How's work?
Ce n'est pas comme ça.	It's not like that.
Vous parlez de quoi?	What are you talking about?
Je ne sais pas.	I don't know.
C'est une bonne question.	That's a good question.
Je dois y aller.	I must go.
Restez en contact.	Keep in touch.
Je reviens tout de suite.	I'll be right back.

Casual French

If you speak casually in English, why not do the same in French? Here are some casual French expressions that you may find handy but always keep in mind that many of these should be reserved for informal conversations.

N'importe quio.	Whatever.
Ça vous dit? / Ça te dit?	You up for it?
Tiens-moi au courant.	Keep me up to date.
T'sais?	You know?
Ouais, enfin ...	Yeah, well ...
Tu t'en sors?	Doing okay there?
Tu fais quoi?	Whatcha doin'?
Ça roule?	How's life?
Laisse tomber.	Forget it.

Chapter 11: Shopping

Who doesn't like shopping? Arm yourself with these words and phrases so that shopping in the French-speaking world can be an enjoyable and pleasant experience.

Je vais faire du shopping.	I'm going shopping.
Pourriez-vous m'aider, s'il vous plaît?	Could you please help me?
Je regarde juste.	I'm just looking.
Veuillez me montrer?	Would you please show me?
Où puis-je trouver ...?	Where can I find ...?
Où est-ce qu'il y a ...?	Where is (are) ...?
Vendez-vous ...?	Do you sell ...?
Je cherche ...	I'm looking for ...
Y a-t-il des soldes?	Are there any sales?
Y a-t-il des rabais?	Are there any discounts?
Combien ça coûte?	How much does it cost?
C'est trop cher.	It's too expensive.
C'est vraiment pas cher.	It's very cheap.

Clothes

English	French	Pronuciation
bathing suit	le maillot de bain	*luh-may-yo-dhaN*
boots	les bottes	*lay-boht*
brassière	le soutien-gorge	*luh-soo-tyaN-gohrzh*
dress	la robe	*lah-rohb*
gloves	les gants	*lay-gahN*
hat	le chapeau	*luh-shah-po*
jacket	la veste	*lah-vehst*
jeans	le jean	*luh-zheen*

negligee	le peignoir	*luh-peh-nywahr*
pajamas	le pyjama	*luh-pee-zhah-mah*
panties	la culotte	*lah-kew-loht*
pants	le pantalon	*luh-pahN-tah-lohN*
raincoat	l'imperméable	*laN-pehr-may-ahbl*
robe	la robe de chambre	*lah-rohb-duh-shahNbr*
scarf	l'écharpe	*lay-shahrp*
shirt	la chemise	*lah-shuh-meez*
shoes	les chaussures	*lay-sho-sewr*
skirt	la jupe	*lah-zhewp*
sneakers	les tennis	*lay-tay-nees*
socks	les chaussettes	*lay-sho-seht*
suit (for men)	le complet	*luh-kohN-pleh*
suit (for women)	le tailleur	*luh-tah-yuhr*
tie	la cravat	*lah-krah-vaht*

About the Fit

Esc-ce-que je peux l'essayer? / Puis-je l'essayer?	Can I try it on?
Je vais essayer cette robe.	I'm going to try on this dress.
Où sont les cabines?	Where are the fitting rooms?
Je porte du petit / moyen / grand.	I wear small / medium / large.
Je chausse du ... + size.	I wear shoe size ...
C'est un peu large.	It's a bit loose.
C'est un peu serré.	It's a little tight.
C'est trop court.	It's too short.
C'est trop long.	It's too long.
Avez-vous de plus grandes tailles?	Do you have a bigger size?
Avez-vous des tailles plus petites?	Do you have a smaller size?

Avez-vous quelque chose ...?	Do you have something ...?
d'autre	else
de plus long	longer
de plus court	shorter
de moins cher	cheaper
de plus cher	more expensive
de meilleure qualité	better
Avez-vous en un neuf?	Do you have a new one?
Je voudrais la voir en blanc.	I'd like to see it in white.
Ça me va.	It suits me.
C'est agréable.	It's nice.
Cette écharpe me plaît beaucoup.	I really like this scarf.
Ça ne me plaît pas.	I don't like it.
Je vais y réfléchir.	I'll think about it.

Colors

Avez-vous d'autres couleurs?			Do you have a different color?		
black	noir(e)	*nwahr*	pink	rose	*roz*
blue	bleu(e)	*bluh*	purple	mauve	*mov*
brown	brun(e)	*bruhN*	red	rouge	*roozh*
gray	gris(e)	*gree(z)*	white	blanc(he)	*blahN(sh)*
green	vert(e)	*vehr(t)*	yellow	jaune	*zhon*
orange	orange	*oh-rahNzh*			

Add the word *clair* after the name of the color to describe it as light. Add the word *foncé* to describe a color as dark.

light green	vert clair
dark blue	bleu foncé

Design and Materials

English	French	Pronunciation
in a solid color	uni(e)	*ew-nee*
in plaid	en tartan	*ahN-tahr-tahN*
checked	à carreaux	*ah-kah-ro*
with stripes	à rayures	*ah-rah-yewr*
with polka dots	à pois	*ah-pwah*
cashmere	en cachemire	*ahN-kahsh-meer*
cotton	en coton	*ahN-koh-tohn*
flannel	en flanelle	*ahN-flah-nehl*
lace	en dentelle	*ahN-dahN-tehl*
leather	en cuir	*ahN-kweer*
silk	en soie	*ahN-swah*
suede	en daim	*ahN-daN*
wool	en laine	*ahN-lehn*

Paying

Je vais prendre ça / ces.	I will take this / these.
Prenez-vous les cartes de crédit?	Do you accept credit card?
Ja paye en liquide.	I'm paying in cash.
Pouvez-vous m'ecrire la recette?	Can you write down the price?
Où est-ce que je peux payer? / Où puis-je payer?	Where can I pay?
Où est la caisse?	Where's the cashier?
Je ne veux pas de sac.	I don't want a bag.
Puis-je avoir un sac?	Can I have a bag?
Pouvez-vous me l'emballer?	Can I have it wrapped?
J'ai besoin du reçu.	I need the receipt.

Food Shopping

For some people, shopping for food may not be as exciting as shopping for new clothes. But in a French-speaking country, you may find shopping for culinary delights a joyful experience.

French Food Shops

French	Pronunciation	English
une boulangerie	*ewn-boo-lahNzh-ree*	bakery
une boucherie	*ewn-boosh-ree*	butcher shop
dairy store	*une crémarie*	dairy store
une charcuterie	*ewn-sharh-kew-tree*	delicatessen
un grand magasin	*uhN-grahN-mah-gah-zaN*	department store
une fruiterie	*ewn-frwee-tree*	fruit store
une épicerie	*ewn-ay-pees-ree*	grocery store
un magasin de vins	*uhN-mah-gah-zaN-duh-vaN*	liquor store
un marché	*uhN-mahr-shay*	market
une pâtisserie	*ewn-pah-tees-ree*	pastry shop
un supermarché	*uhN-sew-pehr-mahr-shay*	supermarket

The preposition *chez,* which means at the house/business of, is commonly used to express where you're going.

Je vais chez l'épicier.	I'm going to the grocery store.
Nous allons chez Jack.	We're going to Jack's house.

All the Food You Can Buy

English	French	Pronunciation
carrot	la carotte	*lah-kah-roht*
cauliflower	le chou-fleur	*luh-shoo-fluhr*
cucumber	le concombre	*luh-kohN-kohNbr*
corn	le maïs	*luh-mah-ees*
eggplant	l'aubergine	*lo-behr-zheen*
lettuce	la laitue	*lah-lehtew*
peas	les petits pois	*lay-puh-tee-pwah*
pepper	le piment	*luh-pee-mahN*
potato	la pomme de terre	*lah-pohm-duh-tehr*
tomato	la tomate	*lah-toh-maht*
apple	la pomme	*lah-pohm*
banana	la banane	*lah-bah-nahn*
coconut	la noix de coco	*lah-nwah-duh-koh-ko*
grape	la raisin	*luh-reh-zaN*
lime	le citron vert	*luh-see-trohN-vehr*
pineapple	l'ananas	*lah-nah-nah*
plum	la prune	*lah-prewn*
strawberry	la fraise	*lah-frehz*
watermelon	la pastèque	*lah-pahs-tehk*
chopped meat	le viande hachée	*luh-vyahNd-ah-shay*
ham	le jambon	*luh-zhahN-bohN*
spareribs	les basses côtes	*lay-bahs-kot*
chicken	le poulet	*luh-poo-leh*
goose	l'oie	*lwah*
turkey	la dinde	*lah-daNd*
crab	le crabe	*luh-krahb*
lobster	le homard	*luh-oh-mahr*
oyster	l'huître	*lwee-truh*
salmon	le saumon	*luhs-so-mohN*
shrimp	la crevette	*lah-kruh-veht*
squid	le calmar	*luh-kahl-mahr*

tuna	le thon	*luh-tohN*
cheese	le fromage	*luh-froh-mahzh*
bread	le pain	*luh-paN*
cake	le gâteau	*luh-gah-to*
cookie	le biscuit	*luh-bees-kwee*
doughnut	le beignet	*luh-beh-nyeh*
French bread	la baguette	*lah-bah-geht*
pie	la tarte	*lah-tahrt*
roll	le petit pain	*luh-puh-tee-paN*
candy	les bonbons	*lay-bohN-bohN*
mineral water	l'eau minérale	*lo-mee-nay-rahl*

Getting the Right Amount

Note that in France, they use the metric system. A kilo is a little more than two pounds. A liter is a bit more than a quart.

English	French	Pronunciation
a bag of	un sac de	*uhN-sahk-duh*
a bar of	une tablette de	*ewn-tah-bleht-duh*
a bottle of	une bouteille de	*ewn-boo-tehy-duh*
a box of	une boîte de	*ewn-bwaht-duh*
a can of	une canette de	*ewn-kahn-neht-duh*
a dozen	une douzaine	*ewn-doo-zeh-duh*
a jar of	un bocal de	*uhN-boh-kahl-duh*
a piece of	un morceau do	*uhN-mohr-so-duh*
a slice of	une tranche de	*ewn-trahNsh-duh*

Pourriez-vous me donner une douzaine d'œufs?	Could you give me a dozen eggs?
Une tranche de gâteau au chocolat, s'il vous plait.	A slice of chocolate cake, please.

If you only want a little of something or you're being given too much, use the following expressions:

English	French	Pronunciation
a little	un peu de	*uhN-puh-duh*
a lot of	beaucoup de	*bo-koo-duh*
enough	assez de	*ah-say-duh*
too much	trop de	*tro-duh*

Chapter 12: Going and Eating Out

Life is meant to be enjoyed. Go out, have fun, and eat some good (French) food. In this chapter, you'll learn all the words and expressions you need from dining at a French restaurant to the different responses you can say if you got invited to go out.

At the Restaurant

Impress your friends or family (and the *serveur*, too) with this collection of essential words related to dining at a French restaurant. Although it might be necessary to give them a call first and reserve a table.

Je voudrais réserver une table pour deux personnes pour vendredi soir à huit heures et demie.	I would like to reserve a table for two people for Friday night at 8:30 P.M.

Important Restaurant Terms

French	Pronunciation	English
le petit déjeuner	*luh-puh-tee-day-zhuh-nay*	breakfast
le déjeuner	*luh-day-zhuh-nay*	lunch
le dîner	*luh-dee-nay*	dinner
le goûter	*luh-goo-tay*	early afternoon snack
commander	*koh-mahN-day*	to order
le menu	*luh-muh-new*	fixed-price meal
la carte	*lah-kahrt*	menu
un pourboire	*uhN-poor-bwahr*	tip
l'addition	*lah-dee-syohN*	check, bill
service (non)	*sehr-vees (non)*	tip (not) included

compris	*kohN-pree*	
défense de fumer	*day-fuhNs-day-few-may*	no smoking
bleu	*bluh*	very rare
saignant	*seh-nyahNt*	rare
à point	*ah-pwaN*	medium
bien cuit	*byaN-kwee*	well-done
au jus	*o-zhew*	in its natural juices
pochés	*poh-shay*	poached
le serveur	*sehr-vuhr*	waiter
le/la chef	*luh/lah-shef*	cook

Remember, when you need the menu, ask for *la carte* and not *le menu* unless you want a set meal and don't want to spend time deciding what you're going to eat.

Make sure that you understand what your waiter is asking you as well.

Que voudriez-vous?	What would you like?
Vous avez choisi?	Have you decided?
Qu'est-ce que je vous sers?	What can I get you?
Que prenez-vous?	What are you having?
C'est à votre gout?	Is everything ok?
Vous le/la (les) voulez comment?	How do you want it (them)?

La Carte

Order what you want, not what (you think) you can pronounce right. The following lists French food and culinary terms so you don't get confused and overwhelmed at a restaurant.

French	Pronunciation	Description
aioli	*ah-yoh-lee*	garlic-flavored mayonnaise
bercy	*behr-see*	a fish or meat sauce
blanquette	*blahN-keht*	white wine sauce with creamy egg
crécy	*kray-see*	carrots
daube	*dohb*	a stew, usually beef
Florentine	*floh-rahN-teen*	spinach
forestière	*foh-rehs-tyehr*	wild mushrooms
jardinière	*zhahr-dee-nyehr*	vegetables
parmentier	*pahr-mahN-tyay*	potatoes
périgourdine	*pay-ree-goor-deen*	truffles
Provençale	*proh-vahN-sahl*	a vegetable garnish
véronique	*vay-rohN-neek*	grapes
les hors-d'œuvres	*lay ohr-duhvr*	appetizers
escargots à la bourguignonne	*ehs-kahr-go-ah-lah-boor-gee-nyohn*	snails in garlic-herb butter
pâté	*pah-tay*	pureed liver (or other meat) served in a loaf
le tournedos	*luh-toor-nuh-do*	small fillets of beef
foie gras	*fwah-grah*	fresh (sometimes uncooked) goose or duck liver
quiche Lorraine	*keesh-loh-rehn*	egg custard tart
les soups	*lay-soop*	soups
la bisque	*lah-beesk*	creamy crayfish soup
la bouillabaisse	*lah-boo-yah-behs*	seafood stew
le consommé	*luh-kohN-soh-may*	clear broth

la soupe à l'oignon	*lah-soop-ah loh-nyohN*	onion soup
le velouté	*luh-vuh-loo-tay*	creamy soup
les viandes	*lay-vyahnd*	meats
le bifteck	*luh-beef-tehk*	steak
le chateaubriand	*luh-shah-to-bree-yahN*	a porterhouse steak
la côte de boeœuf	*lah-kot-duh-buhf*	prime rib
les côtes de porc/veau	*lay-kot-duh-pohr/vo*	pork/veal chops
le rosbif	*luh-rohs-beef*	roast beef
les saucisses	*lay-so-sees*	sausages
les herbes, les épices, et les condiments	*lay-zehrb, lay-zay-pees, ay-lay-kohn-dee-mahn*	herbs, spices and condiments
le basilic	*luh-bah-zee-leek*	basil
le beurre	*luh-buhr*	butter
la ciboulette	*lah-see-boo-leht*	chives
l'ail	*lahy*	garlic
le gingembre	*luh-zhaN-zhahNbr*	ginger
le miel	*luh-myehl*	honey
la confiture	*lah-kohN-fee-tewr*	jam, jelly
le citron	*luh-see-trohN*	lemon
le menthe	*lah-mahNt*	mint
l'huile	*lweel*	oil
le persil	*luh-pehr-seel*	parsley
le poivre	*luh-pwahvr*	pepper
le sel	*luh-sehl*	salt
le sucre	*luh-sewkr*	sugar
le vinaigre	*luh-vee-nehgr*	Vinegar

le dessert	luh-dee-sehr	dessert
une bavaroise	ewn-bah-vahr-wahz	Bavarian cream
une bombe	ewn-bohNb	ice cream with several flavors
une charlotte	ewn-shahr-loht	sponge cake and pudding
des œufs à la neige	day-suh ah lah nehzh	meringues in custard sauce
une glace	ewn-glahs	ice cream
un yaourt	uhN-yah-oort	a yogurt
le vin	luh-vaN	wine
le vin rouge / blahN	luh-vaN-roozh	red / white wine
le vin mousseux	luh-vaN-moo-suh	sparkling wine
le champagne	luh-shahN-pah-nyuh	champagne

Ordering Food

Are you ready to order food? Or do you need some recommendation first? Whichever's the case, use the following phrases and questions.

Qu'est-ce que vous recommandez?	What do you recommend?
Quelle est la spécialité du jour?	What is today's specialty?
Quelle est las spécialité de la maison?	What's the house specialty?
Un instant, s'il vous plaît.	One moment, please.
Puis-je commander?	Can I order some food?
Je voudrais ...	I would like ...
Je prendrai ...	I'll have ...

If you have some dietary restrictions or you have specific preference, the following phrases and statements will be handy.

French	Pronunciation	English
Je suis végétarien(ne).	*zhuh-swee-vay-zhay-tah-ryaN(ryen)*	I'm a vegetarian.
Avez-vous des plats végétariens?	*ah-vay-voo-day-plah-vay-zhay-tah-ryen*	Do you have vegetarian food?
Je ne tolère aucun produit laitier.	*zhuh-nuh-toh-lehr-o-kuhN proh-dwee-leh-tyay*	I can't have any dairy products.
Je ne tolère ...	*zhuh-noh-toh-lehr-pah*	I can't have any ...
J'aimerais ça avec ...		I'd like it with ...
J'aimerais ça sans ...		I'd like it without ...
les œufs	*lay-zuh*	eggs
le poisson	*luh-pwah-sohN*	fish
le lait	*luh-leh*	milk
les cacahuètes	*lay-kah-kah-hweht*	peanuts
les crustacés	*lay-kroo-stah-say*	shellfish
les blé	*luh-blay*	wheat

At the Table

Is something missing on your table? Make sure to ask for the right cutlery.

English	French	Pronunciation
Please bring me a ...	Apportez-moi, s'il vous plaît ...	*ah-pohr-tay-mwah-seel voo-pleh*
bowl	le bol	*luh-bohl*
cup	la tasse	*lah-tahs*
dinner plate	l'assiette	*lah-syeht*
fork	la fourchette	*lah-foor-sheht*
knife	le couteau	*luh-koo-to*
teaspoon	la cuiller	*lah-kwee-yehr*
glass	le verre	*luh-vehr*
wine glass	le verre à vin	*luh-vehr-ah-vaN*
saucer	la soucoupe	*lah-soo-koop*
soup dish	l'assiette à soupe	*lah-syeht-ah-soop*
soup spoon	la cuiller à soupe	*lah-kwee-yehr-ah-soop*
napkin	la serviette	*lah-sehr-vyeht*

Sometimes, what you get might not be up to your standards. Tell the waiter what the problem is with the following phrases.

English	French	Pronunciation
is burned	est brûlé(e)	*eh brew-lay*
is cold	est froid(e)	*eh frwah(d)*
is over-cooked	est trop cuit(e)	*eh-tro-kwee(t)*
is too rare	n'est pas assez cuit(e)	*neh-pah-zah-say-kwee(t)*
is too sweet	est trop sucré(e)	*eh-tro-sew-kray*
is too spicy	est trop épicé(e)	*eh-tro-ay-pee-say*
is too salty	est trop salé(e)	*eh-tro-sah-lay*
is tough	est dur(e)	*eh-dewr*
tastes like	a le goût de	*ah-luh-goo-duh*

At the end of your meal, don't forget to ask for the bill.

L'addition, s'il vous plaît.	The check please.

In a Bar or Café

Here's all you need to know when ordering drinks and some more in a bar or café.

Que voulez-vous boire? / Tu veux boire quoi?	What would you like to drink?
Bonjour! Je voudrais ...	Bonjour! I'd like ... please.
une bière	a beer
une bière pression	a draught beer
une bière anglaise	an ale
un panaché	(a mixture of beer and carbonated lemonade)
une bouteille de vin blanc/rouge	a bottle of white/red wine
une vodka	a vodka
un cognac	a brandy
un martini	a martini
un expresso	un expresso
un café	a cup of (black) coffee
un café crème	a cup of coffee with cream
un café noisette	a cup of white coffee
un chocolat chaud	a hot chocolate
un thé	a tea
Sans glaçons s'il vous plaît.	No ice, please.
Avec des glaçons, s'il vous plaît.	Ice please.
Santé!	Cheers!
Cul sec!	Bottoms up!

Une autre bière, s'il vous plaît.	Another beer, please.
Une autre tournée, s'il vous plaît.	Another round, please.
Je suis pompette.	I'm tipsy.
J'ai trop bu.	I had too many drinks.
Je suis saoul(e).	I'm drunk.
Servez-vous encore?	Are you still serving?
J'ai faim. Il est possible de manger?	I'm hungry. Is it possible to eat?

Going Out

Where do you usually spend your leisure time? Where would you like to go?

J'aimerais aller ...	I would like to go ...
à la plage	to the beach
au concert	to a concert
à une discothèque	to a discotheque
au centre commercial	to the mall
au cinema	to the movies
faire une randonnée	to take a hike
au théâtre	to the theater
au bar	to a bar

It's not as much fun going out alone. Why not invite a friend or two to join you?

Voudriez-vous m'accompagner?	Would you like to join me?
Voudriez-vous nous accompagner?	Would you like to join us?

If it's you who got invited to go out, the following phrases will allow you to accept, refuse, or show indifference or indecision.

French	Pronunciation	English
Avec Plaisir.	ah-vehk-pleh-zeer	With pleasure.
Bien entendu. / Bien sûr.	byaN-nahN-tahN-dew / byaN-sewr	Of course.
C'est une bonne idée.	seh-tewn-bohn-ee-day	That's a good idea.
Chouette!	shoo-eht	Great!
D'accord.	dah-kohr	Okay.
Pourquoi pas?	poor-kwah-pah	Why not?
Volontiers!	voh-lohN-tyay	Gladly.
C'est impossible.	seh-taN-poh-seebl	It's impossible.
Ça marche.	sa-mahrsh	That works.
Je n'ai pas envie.	zhuh-nay-pah-zahN-vee	I don't feel like it.
Je ne peux pas.	zhuh-nuh-puh-pah	I can't.
Je ne suis pas libre.	zhuh-nuh-swee-pah-leebr	I'm not free.
Je regrette.	zhuh-ruh-greht	I'm sorry.
Je suis fatigue(e).	zhuh-swee-fah-tee-gay	I'm tired.
Je suis occupé(e)	zhuh-swee-zoh-kew-pay	I'm busy.
Ça depend.	sah day-pahN	It depends.
Ce que tu préfères.	suh-kuh-tew-pray-fehr	Whatever you want.
Je ne sais pas trop.	zhuh-nuh-seh-pah-tro	I really don't know.
Peut-être.	puh-tehtr	Perhaps. Maybe.

Chapter 13: Health Matters

No one wants to get sick or be in an accident. But invariably, people find themselves in those situations. In this chapter, you will learn how to call for help if you're in an emergency and how to explain to a doctor your ailment and condition.

Emergency!

In France, these are the number you should call in case of emergency:

- 112 – Standard number for all emergencies in the EU (like 911 in the US)
- 15 – Ambulance, medical emergencies
- 17 – Police
- 18 – Firefighters (available for medical emergencies and accidents as well)

Au secours!	Help!
Aidez-moi!	Help me!
J'ai eu un accident. Je besoin d'une ambulance.	I've had an accident. I need an ambulance.
Ma localité est ...	My location is ...
Ja besoin d'un docteur (qui parle Anglais).	I need a doctor (who can speak English).
Pouvez-vous m'aider, s'il vous plaît?	Could you help me please?
Je ne peux pas respirer.	I can't breathe.
Il est inconscient.	He is unconscious.
Deux sont blessés.	Two are injured.

Ilnesses and Symptoms

English	French	Pronunciation
allergic reaction	une réaction allergique	ewn-ray-ahk-syohN-al-lehr-zheek
bruise	une contusion	ewn-kohN-tew-zyohN
burn	une brûlure	ewn-brew-lewr
chills	des frissons	day-free-sohN
cough	une toux	ewn-too
cramps	des crampes	day-krahNp
cut	une coupure	ewn-koo-pewr
diarrhea	de la diarrhée	dun-lah-dee-ah-ray
fever	de la fièvre	duh-lah-fyehvr
lump	une grosseur	ewn-groh-suhr
pain	une douleur	ewn-doo-luhr
rash	une éruption	ewn-nay-rewp-syohN
sprain	une foulure	ewn-foo-lewr
swelling	une enflure	ewn-nahN-flewr
wound	une blessure	ewn-bleh-sewr
appendicitis	l'appendicite	lah-pahN-dee-seet
dizzines	le vertige	luh-vehr-teezh
heart attack	une crise cardiaque	ewn-kreez-kahr-dyahk
stroke	une attaque d'apoplexie	ewn-nah-tahk-dah-poh-plehk-see

What Hurts?

Qu'est-ce-qu'il y a? / Qu'est-ce que vos avez?	What's the matter?

In order to answer that question and to tell the doctor what hurts, you'll need to know the names of your body parts first.

Parts of the Body

English	French	Pronunciation
arm	le bras	*luh-brah*
back	le dos	*luh-do*
chest	la poitrine	*lah-pwah-treen*
ear	l'oreille	*loh-rehy*
elbow	le coude	*luh-kood*
eye	l'œil	*luhy*
eyes	les yeux	*lay-zyuh*
face	le visage, la figure	*luh-vee-zahzh, lah-fee-gewr*
finger	le doigt	*luh-dwah*
foot	le pied	*luh-pyay*
hand	la main	*lah-maN*
head	la tête	*lah-teht*
hip	la hanche	*lah-ahNsh*
knee	le genou	*luh-zhuh-noo*
leg	la jambe	*lah-zhahNb*
lip	la lèvre	*lah-lehvr*
mouth	la bouche	*lah-boosh*
nose	le nez	*luh-nay*
neck	le cou	*luh-koo*
shoulder	l'épaule	*lay-pohl*
stomach	l'estomac	*leh-stoh-mah*

throat	la gorge	*lah-gohrzh*
tongue	la langue	*lah-lahNg*
tooth	la dent	*lah-dahN*
wrist	le poignet	*luh-pwah-nyeh*

Use the expression *avoir mal à* + definite article to inform the doctor which part of your body is bothering you.

J'ai mal aux dents.	I've got a toothache.
J'ai mal à la poitrine.	My chest hurts.
J'ai mal de tête terrible.	I have a terrible headache.
J'ai mal à la gorge.	I have a sore throat.

And here are some more phrases that you can use to explain how you feel:

Je ne me sens pas bien.	I don't feel well.
Je me sens malade.	I feel ill.
Je tousse.	I'm coughing.
Je suis constipé(e).	I'm constipated.
J'ai du mal à dormir.	I have problem sleeping.
J'ai de la fièvre.	I have a fever.
J'ai mal partout.	I hurt all over.
J'ai le vertige.	I feel dizzy.
Je me sense faible.	I feel weak.
Je crois que c'est cassé.	I think it's broken.
Je viens de vomir.	I've been vomiting.
Je suis allergique à/au ...	I'm allergic to ...

The Doctor Wants to Know

Depuis combien de temps souffrez-vous?	How long have you been suffering?
Depuis quand souffrez-vous?	Since when have you been suffering?
Ça fait mal quand vous avalez?	Does it hurt when you swallow?
C'est la première fois que ceci vous est arrivé?	Is this the first time it's happened?

Use these phrases to give and ask for more information.

Je suis malade depuis ...	I've been sick since ...
J'ai cette douleur depuis ...	I've had this pain since ...
Ça fait une semaine.	It's been a week.
J'ai fais mes rappels.	I've had vaccinations.
Je prends ...	I'm taking.
C'est contagieux?	Is it contagious?
C'est grave?	Is it serious?
Combien de temps dois-je garder le lit?	How long do I have to stay in bed?
Combien de fois par jour faut-il prendre ce médicament?	How often do I take this medicine?

The Pharmacy

Où est la pharmacie (de garde) la plus proche?	Where's the nearest (24/7) pharmacy?
Pourriez-vous exécuter cette ordonnance, s'il vous plaît?	Could you please fill this prescription?
Avez-vous quelque chose contre un rhume?	Do you have anything for the cold?
Je voudrais du sparadrap, s'il vous plait.	I would like some plasters, please.
Avez-vous du paracétamol?	Do you have paracetamol?

In France, a green cross above the door marks a pharmacy. At the pharmacy, you can get prescription and over-the-counter drugs as well as items for personal hygiene.

English	French	Pronunciation
I'm looking for ...	Je cherche ...	*zhuh-shersh*
alcohol	de l'alcool	*duh-lahl-kohl*
antacid	un anti-acide	*uhN-nahN-tee-ah-seed*
antihistamine	un antihistaminique	*uhN-nahn-tee-ees-tah-mee-neek*
Band-aid	un pansement adhésif	*uhN-pahNs-mahN-ahd-ay-seef*
cleansing cream	une crème démaquillante	*ewn-krehm-day-mah-kee-yahNt*
condoms	des préservatifs	*day-pray-zehr-vah-teef*
cough drops	des pastilles contre la toux	*day-pah-stee-y-kohNtr-lah-too*
cough syrup	le sirop contre la toux	*luh-see-roh-kohNtr-lah-too*
diapers	des couches	*day-koosh*
eye drops	les gouttes pour les yeux	*lay-goot-poor-lay-zyuh*
ice pack	une vessie de glace	*ewn-veh-see-duh-glahs*
laxative	un laxatif	*uhN-lahk-sah-teef*
mouthwash	de l'eau dentifrice	*duh-lo-dahN-tee-frees*
nail clippers	un coupe-ongles	*uhN-koop-ohNgl*
razor (electric)	un rasoir (électrique)	*uhN-rah-zwahr (ay-lehk-treek)*
razor blades	des lames de rasoir	*day-lahm-duh-rah-zwahr*

143

shampoo	du shampooing	*dew-shahN-pwaN*
sleeping pills	des somnifères	*day-sohm-nee-fehr*
soap	une savonnette	*ewn-sah-voh-neht*
tampons	des tampons périodiques	*day-than-pohN-pay-ree-oh-deek*
tissues	des mouchoirs en papier	*day-moosh-wahr-ahN-pah-pyay*
toothbrush	une brosse à dents	*ewn-brohs-ah-dahN*
toothpaste	de la pâte dentifrice	*duh-lah-paht-dahN-tee-frees*
vitamins	des vitamines	*day-vee-tah-meen*

Chapter 14: Travel

Make the most out of your trip with these essential French words and phrases. From the airport to your hotel and all the sites to see, this chapter will make sure that you get to whereever you're going.

At the Airport

English	French	Pronunciation
airline	la ligne aérienne	*lah-lee-nyuh-ahy-ryehn*
airplane	l'avion	*lah-vyohN*
airport	l'aéroport	*lahy-roh-pohr*
aisle	le couloir	*luh-kool-wahr*
arrival	l'arrivée	*lah-ree-vay*
baggage claim area	les bagages	*lay-bah-gahzh*
bathrooms	les toilettes	*lay-twah-leht*
to board	embarquer	*ahN-bahr-kay*
bus stop	l'arrêt de bus	*lah-reh-duh-bews*
car rental	la location de voitures	*lah-loh-kah-syohN-duh-vwah-tewr*
carry-on luggage	les bagages à main	*lay-bah-gahzh-ah-maN*
cart	le chariot	*luh-shah-ryoh*
counter	le comptoir	*luh-kohN-twahr*
customs	la douane	*lah-doo-ahn*
departure	le départ	*luh-day-pahr*
elevators	les ascenseurs	*lay-zah-sahN-suhr*
emergency exit	la sorite de secours	*lah-sohr-tee-duh-suh-koor*
entrance	l'entrée	*lahN-tray*
exit	la sortie	*lah-sohr-tee*

flight	le vol	*luh-vohl*
gate	la porte	*lah-pohrt*
information	manquer le vol	*mahN-kay-lah-vohl*
money exchange	le bureau de change	*luh-bew-ro-duh-shahNzh*
passport control	le contrôle des passeports	*luh-kohN-trohl-day-pahs-pohr*
security check	le contrôle de sécurité	*luh-kohN-trohl-duh-say-kew-ree-tay*
ticket	le billet	*luh-bee-yeh*

Here are some statements and questions which you may need whether you're checking in or you've just landed.

Où est le comptoir?	Where is the counter?
Je voudrais avoir un siège du côté hublot (couloir), s'il vous plaît.	I'd like to have a window (aisle) seat, please.
À quel carrousel puis-je récupérer mes bagages?	At which carousel can I pick up my luggage?

Means of Transport

Travel is all about going places and exploring different sites. Figuring out which bus or train to take and where they're located is already a challenge. Not all the time a taxi is available but even that requires some communication.

The following are the most important words and phrases you need whether you're using public transport or renting your own vehicle.

146

Le Bus

Combien coûte un billet?	How much is the fare?
Où est l'arrêt de bus le plus proche?	Where is the nearest bus stop?
Est-ce que ce bus s'arrête à ...?	Does this bus stop at ...?
J'aimerai m'arrêter à ...	I'd like to get off at ...
Combien de temps dure le trajet jusqu'à ...?	How long is the trip to ...?
Quel est le prochain arrêt?	What's the next stop?

Le Taxi

Où est l'arrêt de taxi le plus proche?	Where's the nearest taxi stand?
Appelez-moi un taxi, s'il vous plaît.	Would you please call me a cab?
Pouvez-vous m'emmener à ...?	Can you take me to ...?
Pouvez-vous mettre le compteur en marche?	Will you please put the meter on?
Arrêtex-vous ici, s'il vous plaît.	Please stop here.
Attendez-moi.	Wait for me.

Le Métro

Où se trouve la station de métro la plus proche?	Where's the nearest subway station?
Comment aller à la station?	How do I get to the station?
Où puis-je acheter un billet?	Where can I buy a ticket?
Quel est le prix du trajet?	How much is the fare?
Quelle est la station?	What station is this?
Quelle est la prochaine station?	What's the next station?
Il reste combien d'arrêts?	How many more stops are there?
Où puis-je obtenir un plan du métro?	Where can I get a subway map?

Ais-je besoin de changer de train?	Do I need to change train?
Quelle ligne s'arrête à ...?	Which line goes to ...?
Un ticket, s'il vous plait.	One ticket, please.
Un carnet, s'il vous plait.	A pack of metro tickets, please.
Où est la sortie?	Where's the exit?
Est-ce le bon sens pour aller à ...?	Is this the right way to go to ...?
un abonnemet	a subscription / pass
un terminus	last stop
souterrain	underground
une rame	subway train
des escaliers	stairs
des escaliers roulants	escalators
En Travaux	Under Repair/Construction
"En cas d'affluence, ne pas utiliser les strapontins."	"In case of crowded conditions, please don't use the fold-down seats."
Places Prioritaires	Reserved Seats

Le Train

Où est la gare la plus proche?	Where's the nearest train station?
Je voudrais réserver une place.	I'd like to reserve a seat.
Je voudrais un billet de première (deuxième) classe.	I'd like a first- (second-) class ticket.
De quel quia part-il?	From which platform does it leave?
Est-ce que c'est le bon quai pour ...?	Is this the right platform for ...?
Est-ce un train direct?	Is it a direct train?
Où est la voiture-bar?	Which carriage is for dining?
Pouvez-vous me donner les	Can you give me a timetable?

148

horaires des trains?	
A quelle heure part le train pour ...?	What time does the train leave for ...?
un billet simple	one-way ticket
un aller retour	round-trip ticket
les guichets	ticket counter
heure d'arrivée (de départ)	arrival (departure) time
un compartiment (non) fumeurs	a (non) smoking compartment
contrôle des tickets	ticket verification

La Voiture

Je voudrais louer une voiture.	I'd like to rent a car.
Voici mon permis de conduire.	Here's my driving license.
Quel est le tarif à la journée (à la semaine)?	How much does it cost per day (per week)?
Est-ce que ça inclut une assurance?	Does it include insurance?
Quel est le montant de l'assurance?	How much is the insurance?
Le carburant est compris?	Is the gas included?
Qu'est-ce qu'elle prend du diesel ou de l'essence?	Does the car take diesel or petrol?
Est-elle equipée d'un système de GPS?	Does it have GPS?
Acceptez-vous des cartes de crédit? Lesquelles?	Do you accept credit cards? Which ones?
Quan dois-je la rendre?	When do I have to return it?
Est-ce que nous pouvons la laisser à votre agence à ...?	Can we leave it at your agency in ...?
Stationnement Interdet / Défense de Stationner	No Parking
Cédez la Priorité	Give Way

Entrée	Entrance
Sortie	Exit
Ralentissez	Slow Down
Sens Interdet	No Entry
Sens Unique	One Way
Deviation	Detour
Péage	Toll
Douaanne zoll	Border Crossing / Customs
Interdiction de Doubler	No Overtaking
Suivez les panneaux	Follow the signs
La voiture est tombée en panne.	The car has broken down.
La voiture ne démerre pas.	The car won't start.
Le pneu est à plat.	The tire is flat.
Où est-ce qu'il y a une station-service.	Where's a service station.
Je suis en panne d'essence.	I've run out of petrol
Le plein, s'il vous plaît.	Please fill it up.
Est-ce que je peux stationner ici?	Can I park here?

Hotels and More

Vous parlez Anglais? (Do you speak English?) You will likely find at least on person in your hotel who understands and can speak English. But if you like to stay at places that are less-touristy, you'll definitely need more French. Besides, locals will appreciate it if you (try to) communicate in their own language.

The Hotel Room

English	French	Pronunciation
air conditioning	la climatisation	*lah-klee-mah-tee-zah-syohN*
ashtray	un cendrier	*uhN-sahN-dree-yay*
balcony	un balcon	*uhN-bahl-kohN*
bar of soap	une savonnette	*ewn-saah-voh-neht*
bathroom	une salle de bains	*ewn-sahl-duh-baN*
bathtub	la baignore	*lah-beh-nwar*
bed	le lit	*luh-lee*
blanket	une couverture	*ewn-koo-vehr-tewr*
door	la porte	*lah-pohr*
hair dryer	un sèche-cheveux	*uhN-sehsh-shuh-vuh*
hangers	des cintres	*day-saNtr*
key	une clé	*ewn-klay*
mirror	un miroir	*uhN-mee-rwahr*
pillow	un oreiller	*uhN-noh-reh-yay*
safe	un coffre	*uhN-kohfr*
shower	une douche	*ewn-doosh*
single room	une chambre à un lit	*ewn-shahNbr-ah-uhN-lee*
double room	une chambre à deux lits	*ewn-shahNbr-ah-duh-lee*
sink	le lavabo	*luh-lah-va-boh*
sofa	le canapé	*luh-kah-na-pay*
tissues	des mouchoirs en papier	*day-moo-shwahr-ahN-pah-pyay*
(a roll of) toilet paper	un rouleau de papier hygiénique	*uhN-roo-lo-duh-pah-pyay-ee-zhyay-neek*
toilet	la toilette	*lah-twa-leht*
a towel	une serviette	*ewn-sehr-vyeht*

Amenities and Services

English	French	Pronunciation
bar	le bar	*luh-bahr*
bellhop	le bagagiste	*luh-bah-gah-zheest*
concierge	le (la) concierge	*luh-(lah)-kohN-syehrzh*
doorman	le portier	*luh-pohr-tyay*
elevator	l'ascenseur	*lah-sahN-suhr*
maid service	la gouvernante	*lah-goo-vehr-nahNt*
staircase	l'escalier	*lehs-kahl-yay*
swimming pool	la piscine	*lah-pee-seen*
valet parking	l'attendance du garage	*lah-than-dahNs-dew-gah-rahzh*

Note that in French buildings, the ground floor is called *le rez-de-chaussée* (which literally means "level with the road"). The basement is called *le sous-sol*. The first floor that you're used to is actually on the second story of the building.

I Have a Reservation

J'ai une réservation.	I have a room reservation.
J'aimerais faire le check-in.	I'd like to check in.
À quelle heure est le check-out?	What is the check-out time?
À quelle heure est le petit déjeuner?	When is breakfast served?
Est-ce que je peux changer de chambre?	Can I change room?
J'ai laissé la clef dans ma chambre.	I left my key in the room.
Avez-vous du wi-fi?	Do you have wi-fi?
Quel est le mot-de-passe?	What's the password?
Offrez-vous un service de chambre?	Do you have room service?

Pouvez-vous nous conseiller un bon restaurant?	Can you recommend a good restaurant?
Pouvez-vous m'appeler un taxi, s'il vous plaît?	Can you call a taxi for me, please?
Pourriez-vous me réveiller par téléphone à ...	Could you give me a wake-up call at ...?
Je voudrais régler mon compte.	I'd like to pay my bill.
C'est combien?	How much is it?
Est-ce que je peux laisser mes baggages ici?	Can I leave my bags here?
J'aimerais faire le check-out.	I'd like to check-out.
J'ai passé un très bon séjour, merci.	I had a great time. Thank you.

When Something's Not Right

Pourriez-vous changer les draps?	Could you change the sheets?
... ne fonctionne pas.	The ... doesn't work.
Pouvez-vous réparer la toilette?	Can you fix the toilet?
Il n'y a pas d'eau chaude.	There's no hot water.
Veuillez m'envoyer ...	Please send me ...
Il fait trop chaud / froid dans la chambre.	The room is too hot / cold.
J'ai perdu mes clés.	I've lost my keys.

I Don't Have a Reservation

In case you don't have a reservation, or you're looking for another room during your vacation, the following will be quite useful.

Pouvez-vous me recommander un bon l'hotel?	Can you recommend a good hotel?
Où est-ce qu'on peut trouver un hôtel pas cher?	Where can I find a cheap hotel?
Où se trouve ... la plus proche?	Where is the nearest ...?
Est-ce que vous pourriez écrire l'adresse, s'il vous plaît?	Could you write the address, please?
J'ai une réservation.	I don't have a reservation.
Avez-vous une chambre libre pour ce soir?	Do you have a room for tonight?
Avez-vous une chambre simple / double / jumeaux?	Do you have a single / double / twin room?
Pouvons-nous avoir un lit supplémentaire?	Could we add an extra bed?
C'est combien la nuit?	How much is it per night?
Le petit déjeuner est-il inclus?	Is breakfast included?
Y a-t-il une salle de bain?	Is there en-suite bathroom?
Y a-t-il la climatisation dans la chambre?	Does the room have air conditioning?
Y a-t-il l'eau chaude?	Is there hot water?
Y a-t-il du chauffage?	Is there heating?
Est-ce que je peux la voir?	May I see it?
Pourrais-je voir une chambre double?	Can I see a double room?
Puis-je échanger de la monnaie ici?	Can I change money here?
Puis-je utiliser la lavarie / la cuisine?	Can I use the laundry / the kitchen?
Y a-t-il accès à internet ici?	Is there internet here?
Je ne sais pas combien de temps je vais rester.	I don't know how long I'll be staying.
Je vais la prendre.	I'll take it.

If you're looking for something other than the usual *l'hotel,*
here are your other options:

French	Pronunciation	Description
Auberges	*o-behrzh*	roadside inns popular to people travelling by car
Auberge de jeuness	*o-behrzh-duh-zhuh-nehs*	youth hostel where rooms are usually shared (dormitory-type)
Chambres d'hôte	*shaNbr dot*	bed and breakfasts usually in the owner's house in small towns and villages
Gîtes ruraux	*zheet-roo-ro*	private homes or apartments for rent
Motels	*mo-tehl*	common at the airport and near main roads in areas outside large cities
Pensions	*pahN-syohN*	family-run businesses offering a cozy and comfortable atmosphere, ideal for travelers who want to take the path less traveled

Dining Out Options

| J'ai faim. Où devrions-nous manger? | I'm hungry. Where should we eat? |

Words and phrases related to eating at a restaurant are already covered in Chapter 12. Here's a list of establishments that can accommodate your hunger if you're not in the mood for a formal restaurant.

French	Pronunciation	Description
une auberge	*ewn-o-behrzh*	restaurant attached to a roadside inn
un bistro	*uhN-bees-tro*	small informal neighborhood tavern or pub
une brasserie	*ewn-brahs-ree*	large café with relaxed setting that serves quick meals
un café	*uhN-kah-fay*	small neighborhood restaurants that are popular to residents
un cafetéria, un self	*uhN-kah-fay-tay-ryah, uhN-sehlf*	self-service restaurants
une casse-croûte	*ewn-kahs-krot*	snack-house, usually serves sandwiches
une crêperie	*ewn-krehp-ree*	a restaurant or stand that serves crêpes
un fast-food	*uhN-fahst-food*	fast food chain restaurant

Sight-seeing

Whether you decide to DIY or join a group tour, you'll need the following phrases.

Où est l'office du tourisme?	Where's the tourist office?
Qu'est-ce qu'il y a à voir?	What's there to see?
Où puis-je acheter une carte?	Where can I buy a map?
À quelle heure ouvre-t-il?	At what time does it open?
À quelle heure ferme-t-il?	At what time does it close?
Quel es le tarif?	What's the admission price?
On peut fair des photos?	Is it okay to take photos?
Il me fait un guide qui parle anglais.	I need an English-speaking guide.
Combien prend-il?	How much does he charge?
Où y a-t-il des visites guidées?	Where are there guided tours?

Places to Go

Je voudrais aller (I'd like to go) ...

English	French	Pronunciation
to the amusement park	au parc d'attractions	*o-pahrk-dah-trahk-syohN*
to the bridge	au pont	*o-pohN*
to the carnival	au carnaval	*o-kahr-nah-vahl*
to the castle	au château	*o-shah-to*
to the cathedral	à la cathédrale	*ah-lah-kah-tay-drahl*
to the church	à l'église	*ah-lay-gleez*
to the circus	au cirque	*o-seerk*
to the flea market	au marché aux puces	*o-mahr-shay-o-pews*

to the fountain	à la fontaine	*ah-lah-fohN-tehn*
to the garden	au jardin	*o-zhahr-daN*
to the lake	au lac	*o-lak*
to the museum	au musée	*o-mew-zay*
to the nightclub	au cabaret	*o-kah-bah-reh*
to the old city (town)	à la vieille ville	*ah-lah-vyay-veel*
to the public square	à la place	*ah-lah-plahs*
to the river bank	à la rive	*ah-lah-reev*
to the ruins	aux ruines	*o-rween*
to the tower	à la tour	*ah-lah-toor*
to the zoo	au zoo	*o-zo*

If you want to suggest a place that you should visit, use the following expressions.

On va à ...?	How about going to ...?
Allons à...	Let's go to ...
Je voudrais aller à ... Qu'en penses-tu?	I'd like to go to ... What do you think?

I'm Lost

When exploring a new place, it's normal to take some wrong turns, be confused about the directions, or get completely lost. Don't panic. Knowing the following words and phrases will make sure that you'll be back on the right track and reach your destination in no time.

Excusez-moi. Je me suis perdu. Pouvez-vous m'aider?	Excuse me. Can you help me? I'm lost.
Où se trouve ...?	Where is ...?
Est-ce que vous savez où ...?	Do you know where ... is?
Comment y aller?	How do I get there?

158

Est-ce loin?	How far is it?
Pouvez-vous me montrer où c'est sur la carte?	Can you show me where it is on the map?

To understand the replies that you'll get when you ask for help, you should be familiar with the following verbs:

French	Pronunciation	English
aller	*ah-lay*	to go
continuer	*kohN-tee-new-ay*	to continue
descendre	*day-sahNdr*	to go down
marcher	*mahr-shay*	to walk
monter	*mohN-tay*	to go up
passer	*pah-say*	to pass
prendre	*prahNdr*	to take
tourner	*toor-nay*	to turn
traverser	*trah-vehr-say*	to cross

And here are some of the directions that will be given to you.

Allez tout droit sur troix-cents mètres.	Go straight ahead for 300 metres.
Tournez à gauche.	Turn left.
Tournez à droite.	Turn right.
Il se trouve au bout de la rue.	It's at the end of the road.
C'est loin.	It's far.
C'est près d'ici.	It's near.
Prenez la rue / le boulevard ...	Take ... street.
Traversez le pont / la rue.	Cross the bridge / the street.
Continuez jusqu'au feu.	Continue until the traffic lights.
au nord	to the north
au sud	to the south

à l'est	to the east
à l'ouest	to the west
devant	in front of
derrière	behind
à l'opposé	opposite
près de	near
au coin	at the corner
Aller en taxi.	Go by taxi.

Conclusion

I'd like to thank you and congratulate you for transiting my lines from start to finish.

I hope this book was able to help you to speak and understand the French language. If you're someone who wanted to brush up on their French, I hope that you learned more and got to improve your French.

The next step is to put whatever you learned into practice. The best way to learn a language is to try it out so find a French person or anyone who speaks the language fluently and converse with them. Don't be afraid if you make mistakes. You'll only get better if those mistakes are corrected. And the more you practice, the faster you'll learn.

Learn new words everyday. Label all the things you regularly use at home or in your office. Join any activities that can give you the chance to communicate in French. Read articles and children's stories in French even if you don't understand everything. Wathc French movies or TV shows with English subtitle. Aside from growing your vocabulary, your ears will get more used to the sound of spoken French.

Practice everyday and you'll be speaking fluent French sooner than you expect to.

I wish you the best of luck!

Made in the USA
Coppell, TX
15 June 2021

57422986R00089